Teen's Guide to
FACE TO FACE
CONNECTIONS

in a SCREEN-TO-SCREEN WORLD

40 TIPS TO MEANINGFUL *COMMUNICATION*

JONATHAN McKEE
& ALYSSA McKEE

SHILOH RUN PRESS
An Imprint of Barbour Publishing, Inc.

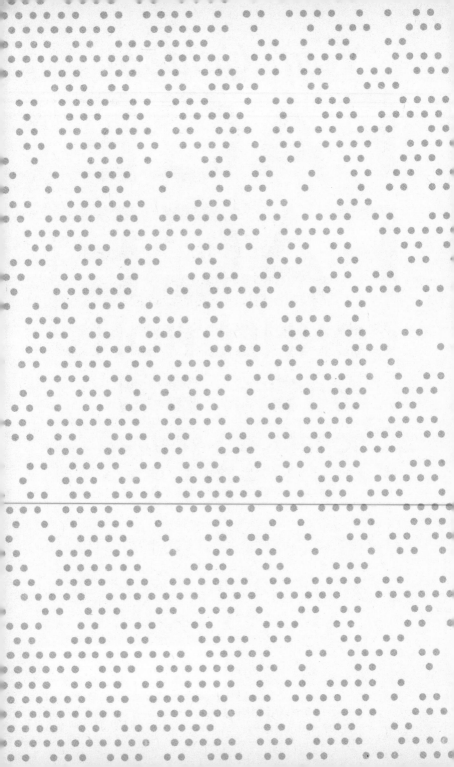

Praise for *The Teen's Guide to Face-to-Face Connections in a Screen-to-Screen World*

"Smartphones and social media dominate daily life and prevent people from making meaningful, face-to-face connections—*but only if we let them*. Youth culture expert Jonathan McKee and his daughter, Alyssa, give excellent advice on how to take control of our devices and start enjoying real, authentic relationships."

–Jim Daly, President of Focus on the Family

"I have been a fan of Jonathan McKee's ministry for a long time. His practical advice wrapped in awesome humor and hard-hitting truth has helped our family navigate the craziness of the digital age. As a pastor who is passionate about building relationships with Gen Z, I am convinced this book is the key to deep, meaningful conversations that transform our hearts. Alyssa and Jonathan have given parents and pastors a phenomenal gift. This book lays out a road map to real parent-child connections that will last a lifetime. The good news is we don't have to throw away our iPhones, unsubscribe to Netflix, or cancel our social media accounts. But, we must embrace the powerful truth that face-to-face is better!"

–Chris Brooks, National Radio Host - Equipped with Chris Brooks, Senior Pastor Woodside Bible Church

"Given generational differences, navigating screens in relationships can be one of the toughest challenges for families today. I'm thankful for Jonathan and Alyssa, father and daughter, for writing a well-researched, honest, and practical guide for building healthy relationships in our screen-based world. This book is a godsend."

–Sean McDowell, PhD, Biola University Professor, Speaker, and Author of over 15 books including *So the Next Generation Will Know*

"Once upon a time, we had face-to-face conversations. But the explosion of screens—*especially* our smartphones—has radically changed how we relate to one another. If you've noticed this tendency in your life and would like to make some changes, Jonathan and Alyssa McKee's book is for you. They'll help you understand how we got here. And through their fun and accessible stories, they'll offer concrete ideas on what it takes to make changes that stick, to once again discover why face-to-face communication is so much more satisfying than the screen-to-screen substitute we sometimes settle for instead."

–Adam R. Holz, Director of *Plugged In*, Focus on the Family's media and technology discernment website

"Jonathan's latest book may be one of his best yet. . .in part, due to the team effort of him and Alyssa. They each bring an incredible amount of experience and wisdom wrapped up in an intergenerational volley of ideas, stories, and challenges that allow every reader to connect and learn. In a world that has become more distant, the need for actual face time becomes critical to the health of our relationships."

–Don Talley, Associate Vice President, YFC USA

"*The Teen's Guide to Face-to-Face Connections* is highly relevant and tailor-made to meet young Christians where they're at. By addressing head-on the broad impact of technology on young people and their relationships, Jonathan and Alyssa challenge readers to notice the world beyond their screens and experience the freedom and joy of genuine relationships."

–Greg Stier, Founder and CEO of Dare 2 Share

"If ever there was a need for a one-of-a-kind book to help develop real connections in a virtual world, now is that time. Jonathan is already my go-to-guy for anything related to young Christians and the culture they're navigating, and now he's partnered with his daughter, Alyssa, to write an important, accessible guidebook. *The Teen's Guide to Face-to-Face Connections* is written from two unique generational perspectives and will immediately resonate with parents and teens. If you're looking for some help understanding and living authentically in a world dominated by virtual relationships, this book is for you."

–J. Warner Wallace, Senior Fellow at the Colson Center for Christian Worldview, Author of *Cold-Case Christianity* and *So the Next Generation Will Know*

"Jonathan and Alyssa's book is a sobering peek into my own teenagers' relationship with their screens. Alyssa's confessions about her experience with social media are not only vulnerable and insightful, they will resonate with today's teenagers. Really enjoyed this book, and I know the digitally-concerned parent will enjoy going through it with their teen!"

–Josh Griffin, Co-founder of Download Youth Ministry & Junior High Pastor Mariners Church

"*The Teen's Guide to Face-to-Face Connections* by Alyssa and Jonathan McKee is so timely! In the midst of the largest pandemic in modern history, we are learning even more how important face-to-face connection really is! Not being able to connect with people in person has left me yearning for connection to my loved ones on a deeper level. Jonathan and Alyssa remind us of the importance of being present, especially if that means logging off IG and FB and tapping into real relationships."

–Maggie John, TV Anchor/Producer - Context Beyond the Headlines

"Jonathan McKee's passionate research into the impact of technology on our kids has provided him with a message that every kid and their parents need to hear. Jonathan's newest book, written with his daughter, is refreshing and insightful. Jonathan's knowledge of the subject coupled with his daughter's authenticity are a killer combination providing the perfect resource both parents and kids can read together."

–Bob Johns, Youth Pastor, First Woodway

"Face-to-face friendships and relationships today are more difficult to navigate and engage in than ever before as we live in an online world. Jonathan and Alyssa McKee share their challenges and what they have learned in an inviting way. They offer 40 Realizations and more than 230 questions to help all of us become better in our own personal relationships!"

–Mark W. Kirgiss, Sr. Area Director, Greater Lafayette Young Life

"Youth workers have seen the landscape of youth culture transformed by digital communication. Alyssa and Jonathan capture relevant topics with fun stories that lead readers to participate in constructive conversations with practical wisdom. I personally love the questions in each chapter which can help spark meaningful conversations with young people. You hold in your hands a great resource for intentional discussions to help you enjoy greater face-to-face time with your family!"

–Rev. Wayne Morgan Jr., National Ministries Director, National Network of Youth Ministries

FOR ELISE...
and our future
face-to-face conversations!

Print ISBN 978-1-64352-468-9

eBook Editions:
Adobe Digital Edition (.epub) 978-1-64352-822-9
Kindle and MobiPocket Edition (.prc) 978-1-64352-823-6

Cover Design: Greg Jackson, Thinkpen Design

The author is represented by, and this book is published in association with, the literary agency of WordServe Literary Group, Ltd., www.wordserveliterary.com.

Published by Shiloh Run Press, an imprint of Barbour Publishing, Inc., 1810 Barbour Drive, Uhrichsville, Ohio 44683, www.shilohrunpress.com.

Our mission is to inspire the world with the life-changing message of the Bible.

Member of the
Evangelical Christian
Publishers Association

Printed in the United States of America.

Contents

440 Miles Apart

This book you're holding in your hands is pretty unique. It's a collection of observations and insights from two minds. . .two very *different* minds from two completely different generations.

Alyssa is in her twenties, working at the college she graduated from and living with a bunch of girls literally across the street from a beach in Southern California.

Jonathan is in his late forties, has written over twenty books, speaks at schools, conferences, and churches around the world, and is living with his wife, Lori, on a few acres at the base of the Sierra Mountains in Northern California.

Alyssa and Jonathan live 440 miles from each other, seven hours apart (six hours, twenty minutes if Jonathan is driving).

Alyssa loves lying on the beach.

Jonathan loves riding his John Deere.

Alyssa drives an adorable little Kia.

Jonathan drives a four-wheel drive.

Alyssa likes sushi.

Jonathan likes pizza and wings.

Alyssa and Jonathan are as different as night and day, which makes this book distinct, especially in that two *completely* different people *completely* agree about one thing:

Face-to-face is better.

It's that simple.

Alyssa and Jonathan both have iPhones, they both binge Netflix occasionally, they're both on Instagram, and sometimes they're both shocked by how many hours of screen time they average during any given week (but let's be real—Alyssa still clocks more than Jonathan).

Yet both have learned that as fun as their screens are...*face-to-face is better*.

No, they're not throwing their phones in the garbage and canceling all their social media accounts (although they each have taken extended breaks). They both enjoy their screens. But interestingly enough, Alyssa and Jonathan, young and old (sorry, Jonathan, you *are* getting some grays), have individually learned that sometimes it's better to put screens away and enjoy the people in the room.

Screen-to-screen can be fun.

But face-to-face is better.

Agreed!

Although it should be noted that Jonathan also agrees that Mexican food is waaaay better in Southern California than in Northern California. And they both eat lots of it!

Like daddy, like daughter.

Enjoy this peek into their creative minds!

I wish I knew.

I really do.

If only I knew then what I know now.

You see, I was born at a unique time and have sat in the front row watching a major transformation take place: the shift from *face-to-face* to *screen-to-screen*. We live in a world where the average mom, the average dad, and the average kid spend more time staring at screens than they do engaging in conversation with each other in person.

Pause and think about that for a second. Most of us spend the majority of our time ignoring the people we care about the most.

Most of us don't mean to do it. Screens just tend to distract.

And face it, we loooove our screens!

It's not your fault. In fact, if you're under twenty right now, then you've never known any different. Screens have always been the dominant form of communication in your life. In fact, all of you have lived through a global pandemic where screens became your *only* form of communication with the outside world. We are a connected generation. Statistically, if you're a teenager, 97 percent of you are on social media,[1] 89 percent of you have a smartphone,[2] 79 percent of you even bring your phone to the bedroom with you each night,[3] 70 percent use it within thirty minutes of going to sleep,[4] and 36 percent wake up at least once during the night to check social media or a notification.[5] Mom and Dad do the same. Sometimes even more so.

But it wasn't always this way. . . .

AWKWARDLY IN THE MIDDLE

I'm just twenty-four years old as I write this. I was born in 1995, smack-dab on the line between generations. So if you hear someone talking about "Millennials" or "Gen Z". . .take your pick. I'm both.

Or neither.

Some say Gen Z began in 1997; others say 1995. No matter which way you look at it, everyone agrees those people born before me experienced something very different than those born after me.

Then there's me, awkwardly in the middle.

Story of my life. (I'm a middle child.) And all my life I've been witnessing this unprecedented change in communication technology, especially as it has affected young people. You see, my dad has always worked with teenagers. We had teenagers at our house since I was a baby, and now I work with teenagers. I'm an admissions counselor at a Christian college in Santa Barbara, and my job involves flying to cities across the US to talk with high school kids about their future college and job opportunities. When I'm not traveling, I'm hanging out with a small group of high school girls at my church where I volunteer as a youth leader. So my whole life I've been watching teenagers communicate with each other. My life is literally a window into the time line of communication gadgetry.

And boy, have things changed.

THE PAGER

When I was a little kid, every teenager I saw—literally every one— had a pager. Pagers were available in every color imaginable. My dad's was green (yes, adults had them too). When teens were over at my house, their pager would vibrate and they'd glance down at the little monochrome LCD display capable of ten digits. Typically, he or she would then ask my dad, "Can I use your phone? I was just paged."

This happened hourly.

Kids desperately wanted to communicate with each other, and they loved the opportunity to be able to beckon each other with ten monochrome digits. Many teens even developed codes so their friends would know who was paging (because their friends might be paging from a pay phone or someone else's house).

Phones were still landlines at the time—like connected to the kitchen wall. Cell phones were available, but only adults had them. Kids were always borrowing my dad's cell phone to return a page.

But here's the thing—teens talked to each other *all the time*. They were either talking on a landline phone or talking in person.

Either way, they *talked*.

But soon cell phone companies began offering free phones as an incentive for committing to a phone service plan. Parents began signing contracts, promising to stay with a certain phone company in exchange for a new Nokia or Motorola flip! Phone plans became much more affordable, and that's when we began to see teenagers with phones.

But teenagers weren't excited about *talking* on their phones anymore. . .they preferred texting!

TEXT ME

In 1999 phones finally allowed SMS (short message service) messages between phone services. By the year 2000 phone owners averaged only 35 texts per month.[6]

Think about that.

That's like one text per day. (I wonder what they said in just one text. What would you send in just one text? *Please bring me Starbucks!*)

Again, back then talking still ruled.

That's because teenagers didn't all have phones in their pockets yet. But once young people got phones, texting exploded. And so did their parents' phone bills!

Phone companies used to charge per text, often 10 cents a text. So once kids started texting, this got very expensive. Picture the typical conversation:

> Whatcha doing?
>
> Nothing. U?
>
> Homework.
>
> Lame.
>
> I know, right?
>
> I'm not doing mine.
>
> Lucky.
>
> Haha. I guess.
>
> C U ltr.
>
> Bring me Starbucks!

That conversation cost a dollar.

And kids would have about ten of those eloquent conversations per day. Soon teenagers averaged over three thousand texts a month.

A $300 phone bill!

Two things happened.

1. Parents were freaking out, yelling at their kids and yelling at the phone companies.

2. Phone companies got tired of getting yelled at, so they began offering "free texting" plans.

Every parent in the world quickly switched to these free texting plans so they didn't get stuck with one of those huge phone bills again. And texting continued to grow, eventually surpassing talk time.

When I got my first phone, I barely ever made phone calls. *I texted.*

And you know my fingers flashed like lightning across that miniscule keypad!

Of course, texting then was using the number keys. It's called T9 texting. That's why we all used "text speak" or abbreviated words. If you wanted to type "See you later," that required typing the following:

S: 7 four times
E: 3 two times
E: 3 two times
SPACE
Y: 9 three times
O: 6 three times
U: 8 two times
SPACE
L: 5 three times
A: 2 one time
T: 8 one time
E: 3 two times
R: 7 three times

That's twenty-eight buttons just to type a twelve-letter sentence! That's why that sentence quickly became C U ltr.

Ask any twentysomething young adult like me. We quickly developed mad phone tapping skills. I could type a response without even looking (and often did, under my desk).

That's what we did on our phones.

We texted. . .

Or played Snake (a dumb game where you maneuvered around the screen eating objects and trying to avoid eating your own tail).

Social media wasn't mobile yet.

FOUR DEVICES INTO ONE

Picture what technology looked like for the typical young person at the time. We had a phone that we used for texting. We had a separate game system like the Wii so we could get our dose of Mario Kart. We had an iPod with all our music on it. And if our parents let us on social media, we did that on a computer that was attached to a wall.

Most of my friends had these four devices: phone, game system, iPod, access to a computer. All those things were separate.

Until 2007.

In 2007 one man changed everything.

In 2007 a guy wearing jeans, a black turtleneck, and white sneakers stood on the stage at Apple and made an announcement that changed the world. He said, "We're gonna make some history together today."[7] And that's exactly what Steve Jobs, the founder and CEO of Apple, did. He changed history as we all know it. He released the first iPhone, combining phone, games, iTunes, and internet access in one device.

Forget four screens—now you only needed one!

And it fits in your pocket.

I was in middle school when this happened, and one by one, my friends began replacing their little texting phones with these new "smartphones." First they were iPhones, but Androids were soon to follow.

People my age remember one thing about the first year of the iPhone: *Angry Birds*. This game was waaaay better than Snake. I would borrow my dad's iPhone as often as possible just to play *Angry Birds*. But as more Americans got iPhones, more teenagers got iPhones, and soon teens wanted more than just *Angry Birds*. They wanted social media on their mobile devices. And in 2012 they got their wish.

FIVE YEARS LATER

I'm not the only one who will tell you that 2012 was an important year for technology. In 2012, only five years after the iPhone was introduced, several shifts occurred:

1. Americans crossed the 50 percent mark for smartphone ownership.[8] Now the majority of people had a smartphone in their pocket. They had mobile access to the internet and social media, so it was no surprise when social media released some very mobile-friendly platforms.

2. Snapchat launched, providing an opportunity for teens to send a message like a text, but with a picture or video. Snapchat became an instant hit in 2012, and the number one communication tool among teens.

3. Instagram became a "thing." Sure, Instagram launched in late 2010.[9] But honestly, no one really knew about it until late 2011, and it wasn't until early 2012 that it came to Android. My friends and I *all* got Instagram in 2012.

In short, 2012 was a landmark date for digital communication. Here's where you'll really see my age as an "in-betweener." The people older than me didn't have social media on their phones growing up. They just had texting. But the people younger than me, like my little sister, Ashley, had social media on their phones most of high school.

But I, the in-betweener, became a senior in high school in August 2012. Snapchat and Instagram were both brand-new. Most of my friends didn't get Snapchat or Instagram until my senior year (2012–2013). And believe me when I tell you, once these two apps were on our phones, communication as we knew it changed.

I saw it firsthand.

Less talking face-to-face. More heads buried in Instagram sending DMs.

Car rides used to be full of conversation. Now people isolated themselves with headphones and social media conversations.

Social media is changing how we value people. The people outside the room are now more important than those inside the room.

Social media has changed how we value ourselves. Our social media "presence" is now a factor that influences our self-esteem. Variables like "friends," "followers," and "likes" actually affect how we feel about ourselves. As if self-image wasn't already difficult enough.

Social media has also given predators a new playground to solicit young people, a playground where they can be whoever they want to be, and way too many young people fall victim to their tricks each year.

Social media is a place where everyone's mistakes are publicized, replayed, critiqued, and commented on over and over and over and over and over and over and over. . .(how many views is that?).

I wonder if those techs at Apple predicted all this when they were designing the first iPhone.

WHAT NOW?

Screens obviously have some drawbacks, especially when not used wisely, but they are not *all* bad. I mean, honestly, I like screens. I use my phone, for example, to connect with family and friends, to do research, and even to read the Bible. My phone can be a big help. . .or a big distraction.

Is there by chance a way to adapt and become more "screen-wise"?

Are there ways to use our phones for healthy connections while being careful not to form unhealthy habits?

Are there ways to define our use of social media without allowing social media to define us?

What does this actually look like?

What would it take to become *socially skillful* in a *dysfunctionally digital* world?

That's exactly why my dad and I wrote this book. We know that you probably enjoy screens, but don't want them hurting your relationships with people who matter. What if you could improve your face-to-face relationships, develop deeper connections, graciously resolve conflict, and confidently communicate with friends, parents, teachers, roommates, coworkers, potential employers. . .even the barista at your local coffee shop!

What if your phone truly helped you *connect* with people more than *disconnect* with those around you?

What if you thought through what you posted, avoiding some of the hurt and consequences that almost always come back to haunt you?

What if you became a master of your own screen time instead of letting it master you?

What if you became more *screen-wise*?

These are some of the lessons I've been learning.

I'll be honest. I've learned many of these lessons the hard way. *Through hurt.*

Experiencing pain and heartache and realizing, "I don't want to experience that again!"

I've also been learning many of these lessons in my work with young people. Every day I see young people navigating these issues, making choices and experiencing the consequences of those choices. Many of them are even evaluating their own smartphone use and screen time. The majority of the kids I work with admit, "I probably spend too much time on my phone."

But they don't know exactly what to do about it.

My dad brings a vault of knowledge on this subject, not only as an author of piles of books and a speaker addressing audiences across the world about teen mental health, but as a dad and a youth worker who actually hangs out with kids with screens.

Let's just say the two of us have learned countless lessons about these screens we cherish so dearly.

The two of us are *still* learning how to become more screen-wise.

If only I knew then—when I got my first smartphone—what I know now.

You don't have to learn the hard way.

You can avoid much of the hurt.

You can steer clear of many of the consequences.

You can become smarter with your smartphone.

Our goal is simply to give you information that helps you navigate these decisions daily.

You can dare to be relationally different in a screen-to-screen culture.

In the chapters to follow, we look at 40 random realizations we've made in our journey over the last five years. We hope they'll help you too.

Random Realizations

Our Journey to Becoming Socially Skillful in a Dysfunctionally Digital World

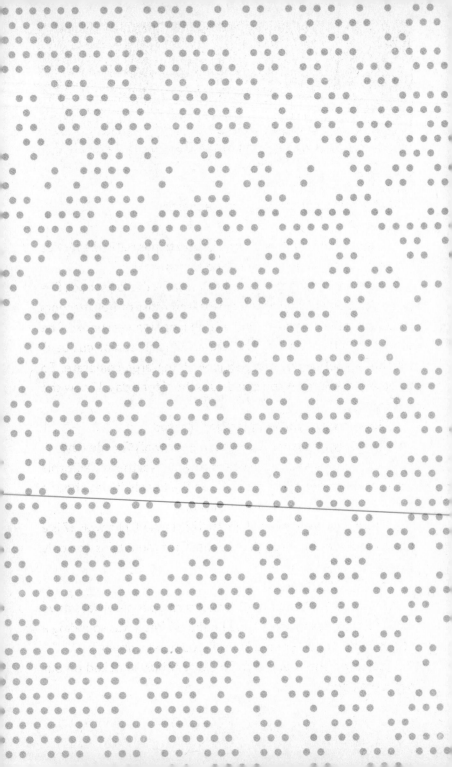

"Dad, I want to cut school next Wednesday."

"Sure."

Okay, I admit, that's not normally how things roll in the McKee house, but you have to understand the context.

Ashley, my youngest, was in her last week of high school. She had a 4.2 GPA, her finals were over, and most of her teachers were just showing movies and letting kids sign yearbooks. The school she attended did not have an official "senior cut day," which is an actual day many schools in our area celebrate. So when Ash asked me if she could cut school for a day, I knew she deserved it.

"So where are you going to go?" I asked.

"Probably the Santa Cruz Beach Boardwalk for the day."

Santa Cruz is a fun little beach town in Northern California with an amusement park set right on the beach. It was about a three-hour drive from where we lived.

"Have you ever driven Highway 17?" I asked. Highway 17 is a curvy road weaving through the Santa Cruz Mountains, the only road from here to there.

"No, why?" she asked.

"It's just a precarious road, lots of turns, people always drive it too fast, constant wrecks and fatalities." Yes, I was sounding a little bit like a dad. "Let me know if you need a driver."

Tuesday night at about ten o'clock Ashley knocked on our bedroom door.

"Dad?" Ashley said through the door. "My friends' parents won't let them go unless an adult drives."

"No problem," I said. "What time do we leave?"

The next morning three of her friends were at our house at six o'clock. The five of us loaded into the car and began our journey toward the coast. This was a fun group of friends. They were in many of the same classes as Ash, and all of them would be heading off to different colleges in the fall.

As I pulled out of the driveway, the phones immediately came out.

It's almost automatic, right? People get in the car and if they *aren't* driving, they check their phones. It's what we do. We've conditioned our brain to crave that little device in our pocket.

It's like this. The first time you scrolled through social media, watched a funny online video, or received a few likes, your brain rewarded you with little shots of dopamine— a chemical released in the reward centers of the brain that helps you remember what feels good doing certain activities, similar to what people experience if they take drugs or play the slots in Vegas. [1] Next time that particular activity is dangled before your senses, dopamine gives you a rush, anticipating the good feeling, drawing you in to do it even more. For that reason, dopamine-triggering behaviors easily become a habit, which is why most studies show *social media leads to more social media*. So you mindlessly begin to pick up your phone without thinking—because that's where the pleasure lies, right? Your brain craves that reward regularly.

App developers know this and use it to draw you to spend even more time on their apps. (If you're curious about this phenomenon, just google the words *dopamine brain smartphone* and you'll discover some fascinating research.)

But do you know what is even more rewarding?

Real-life interpersonal connection.

So as the five of us embarked on our journey, I began asking questions.

"So, Chris, I heard you're going to San Diego State. Beautiful school. What made you decide on that school?"

And the conversation began—not with just one of them, but with *all of them*. They set down their phones one by one as they became immersed in the conversation.

We talked about the schools they'd attend, the jobs they hoped to get, the places they'd live, the things they were scared of—especially leaving home for the first time. Interesting conversation.

I don't know if it was just that we were all dialoguing about fascinating subject matter, or the fact that the roads were pretty windy, but no one—not one person—was looking at their phone. And when we arrived at Santa Cruz, it was no different. We all burst from the car to explore the empty boardwalk, the beach, surf and skate shops, candy stores. . .you name it.

Occasionally someone would pull out their phone to shoot a picture of all of us eating cotton candy off one stick, folding our pizza to fit it in our mouths, or lifting our hands in the air at the top of the first peak of the Giant Dipper, one of the coolest wooden roller coasters still in existence! But if you add up the three-hour drive there, another eight hours at the beach boardwalk, and another three hours driving home, we probably saw phones out for less than thirty minutes (probably a record low for most of us compared to a normal day).

Funny, at the end of the day when I pulled back into our driveway, one of my daughter's friends said, "Wow, this was a lot of fun."

"Of course," I said. "Beach, roller coasters, pizza. Hard to beat that."

"Naw," he said. "That's all good stuff. But I meant the conversation."

Wow. Whodathunkit?

REALIZATION #1: Conversation is far more enjoyable when everyone just puts their phone in their pocket.

. . . .

ASK YOURSELF OR A FRIEND

1. What's one of the funnest days you can remember? (And yes, I know *funnest* isn't actually a word.) What made it so fun?

2. How can our screens add to days like these?

3. How do our screens subtract from days like these?

4. What is a place where you find it's easy to just sit and talk with family or friends?

5. What is something you can plan with your friends or family where screens stay in the pocket for most of the day and you just enjoy good conversation?

FINAL THOUGHTS

Ashley and her friends tasted something on senior cut day that they hadn't tasted in a long time: uninterrupted conversation (and cotton candy).

In a world where most people spend over nine hours a day soaking in entertainment media (9 hours, 49 minutes for teenagers,[2] and 11 hours, 27 minutes for adults[3]—yes, adults clock more than teenagers), there isn't always a lot of time left for face-to-face conversation.

Here's the thing: people typically enjoy face-to-face conversation more. And they typically wish they could soak in more of it.

What about you? What can you do to soak in more face-to-face conversation this week?

Alyssa Writes. . .

CHAPTER 2

Connected Disconnect

I can remember the day I first noticed it.

Sure, I had experienced it before, but something about this day flipped a switch in my brain. It was just a few years ago, and it was probably the day I began this journey of becoming a little more screen-wise.

There I was sitting on my fifty-dollar, stained, Craigslist sofa with two of my roommates staring at a screen.

Actually, four screens—one TV and three phones.

We'd been roommates for almost three months, so the three of us girls watching cheesy rom-coms on weekend nights had become a regular occurrence by now.

Seven minutes into the movie I burst out laughing at a particularly funny scene only to realize. . .*no one else was laughing with me*.

I felt a little foolish.

I peeked at my roommates. They were both entranced by their phones, scrolling through their social media feeds, completely void of expression.

"Did you see that?" I said hopefully, trying to redeem myself by explaining the joke to them. Only I overexplained it, rambling and failing miserably at duplicating the humorous moment.

I paused. An awkward silence followed.

About fifteen seconds later, what seemed like fifteen minutes, one of my roommates awoke from her coma and looked up from her phone. "Oh. . .what?" A glazed expression still on her face.

Just then my other roommate laughed at her screen, sinking back deeper into the couch and smiling to herself, oblivious of everyone.

"Nevermind," I slurred into one word. "It was just a funny scene."

No response. Just more scrolling.

The movie continued, and I began to realize I was the only one really paying attention to the film at all. All three of us could have been in different rooms and it wouldn't have made a difference.

We were all in separate worlds.

And this wasn't a unique occurrence.

Months passed and it happened again and again, not just with these roommates, but with all my friends. It was the norm. Same room, different worlds. We were all together, yet all apart.

These little mobile devices we own and love might have been connecting us with people miles away from us, but they were disconnecting us from the friends sitting right next to us.

Was I the only one experiencing this?

A CULTURAL SHIFT

Apparently I'm experiencing what most of my generation is feeling, something I call *connected disconnect*. We're connected to our devices but disconnected from the people around us.

The smartphone is changing the way we think, process information, digest entertainment, and communicate. Social media expert Dr. Jean Twenge (author of *iGen*) argues that it's changing way more than that: "The arrival of the smartphone has radically changed every aspect of teenagers' lives, from the nature of their social interactions to their mental health."[1]

I can vouch for that. I've seen it happen with my classmates, and now with the high school girls I meet with every week. The more we get used to screen time (and the average teenager soaks in almost 10 hours a day of entertainment media[2]) the less we all spend talking with each other. The less time we talk, the more we become socially inept.

Bottom line: Too much screen time is making us socially stupid.

Eating a meal with a friend? How often do you make it through an entire meal without someone whipping out their phone and ignoring the people around the table?

Road trip? Everyone has on headphones listening to their own playlists.

Talking seriously with a friend and her phone vibrates in her pocket? Does she ignore it. . .or does she peek?

Trying to sleep? You'll average about an hour less if your phone's within reach.

In the bathroom? How many of you know someone who dropped their phone in the toilet? (How many of *you* have dropped your phone in the toilet?)

Our phones are slowly infiltrating *every* area of our lives, and our interpersonal relationships are suffering. Many of us jumped at the opportunity to connect with others through phones, social media, or online gaming, thinking it would make us more social, but in actuality, the pervasive overwhelming connectivity has actually disconnected us from the people close to us—*connected disconnect*.

Humans have a history of allowing "overconnection" to get in the way of our important relationships, even before technology. Jesus experienced this kind of overwhelming "overconnection" at times when the crowds bombarded Him from every side. Like in the Bible in the book of Mark:

> Then Jesus said, "Let's go off by ourselves to a quiet place and rest awhile." He said this because there

were so many people coming and going that Jesus and his apostles didn't even have time to eat. So they left by boat for a quiet place, where they could be alone. (Mark 6:31–32 NLT)

"Where they could be alone."

I find it intriguing that even Jesus needed time to withdraw from the chaos and connect with His disciples. It's not that Jesus *didn't* like crowds of people. He often reached out to crowds. But He also knew the importance of *disconnecting* from the masses at times so He could *connect* with the individuals in front of Him.

Today we do the exact opposite of His wise example. We disconnect from the people in front of us to connect with all our online friends and followers. Don't get me wrong. Online community isn't harmful unless we allow it to disconnect us from the people we see every day.

Sadly, screens and social media are making most people "less social." They are going out less, doing less physical activity, and making fewer face-to-face connections.

I actually already see a huge difference between what my high school girls are experiencing compared to what I experienced in high school—and I'm just twenty-four! But social lives and communication habits have changed completely in just the last five to seven years. It's no longer unusual to ignore the people you care about and retreat to your screens. Kids are becoming less social and less active. The shift is mind-boggling. Twelfth graders in 2015 went out less often than *eighth graders* did as recently as 2009.[3]

The high school closest to my home just canceled its Winter Ball because only sixteen kids bought tickets out of over one thousand students.

Why?

Because everyone was sitting at home watching Netflix.

Is this our future?

It doesn't have to be.

ASK YOURSELF OR A FRIEND

1. Which of Alyssa's examples of "connected disconnect" do you observe in your social circles? (Do you notice people pulling out their phone during meals or conversations, wearing headphones that keep them isolated from others, focusing on screens instead of the people around them, letting their phone keep them up at night, etc.?)

2. Do you find yourself doing any of these?

3. What are the consequences?

4. Why do you think fewer people go out with friends now than just ten years ago?

5. When do you feel most disconnected from your friends and family?

6. What is something you can do to try to reconnect?

FINAL THOUGHTS

A group of friends sitting in a room together scrolling in silence. I couldn't deal with it anymore.

Sitting on my couch alone—well, not really alone, but feeling pretty alone—I had to make a move toward better relationships. But how could I compete with the ever-addicting phone screen?

This was my awakening, the beginning of my journey.

Keep reading. I'll tell you more about it.

CHAPTER 3
Less Is More

I love cheesecake.

Scratch that. I *loved* cheesecake.

Until I had twenty-three pieces of cheesecake in one sitting.

THE BET

When I was nineteen years old, I was poor and a little bit insane.

I was poor because I was a starving college kid and every dime was going into my education. I was insane because. . .*every dime was going into my education!*

This means whenever my friends were going out for pizza, I didn't have enough money to go out for pizza. When they were all going to a movie, I couldn't afford to go to a movie. And that's exactly what set my insanity into motion one particular evening in my college cafeteria. All my friends were going to see a movie, and I knew I couldn't go. So my friend Erik decided to have a little fun with me.

Erik had plenty of money, and he knew I reeeeally wanted to go to a movie with everyone. So he made me a deal.

Erik often made me deals. They always started with the words "I bet. . ."

Erik knew I would do stupid things for money. So he began looking around the cafeteria and said, "I bet you wouldn't. . ."

Erik's eyes stopped at the dessert bar. The dessert bar had hundreds of pieces of cheesecake laid out.

I loved cheesecake!

"I bet you wouldn't eat. . ." Erik pondered his words. "I bet you wouldn't eat twenty-three pieces of cheesecake!"

I didn't even hesitate.

"Deal!"

My friends all began collecting pieces of cheesecake and I started wolfing them down.

And they were delicious. . .for about the first ten minutes.

Then they started tasting bland.

Like lard.

Like phlegm!

Like. . .*disgusting*!

I won't give you all the gory details, but let's just say that I only threw up once and then kept eating until I shoved all twenty-three pieces of cheesecake down.

On one hand, I got to go see the movie with my friends. But honestly, I don't even remember the movie. I just remember hating that my stomach felt like I had just eaten a water buffalo. Maybe even two.

So much for my love for cheesecake.

And that's just the thing. All good things are good. . .in moderation.

Even our phones.

Our phones and other screens can be really fun. . .when we don't let them enslave us. But chances are you might already be feeling symptoms of this. **If you're like most of today's young people, you enjoy your devices, but you recognize that too much of this good thing is *not* a good thing!**

Last year a bunch of researchers asked teenagers their opinions about their own screen time. I think some people were surprised to discover how teenagers really feel about their devices:

- Nine in ten teenagers view spending too much time online as a problem facing people their age, including 60 percent who say it is a major problem.[1]

- 54 percent of teenagers think they spend too much time on their phone.[2]
- Almost 70 percent of teenagers surveyed admitted that they wish they could spend more time "socializing face-to-face" than online.[3]

It's not that these teenagers saw their devices as harmful or evil—they just realized that too much time online, too much time on their phone, and too much screen-to-screen communication was a problem.

These young people simply discovered that *less is more.*

That's what I learned the hard way about cheesecake.

It's amazing how easy it is to make excuses for our actions. Long ago people were making excuses like this to the apostle Paul, basically telling him, "I'm allowed to do anything, right?" because they knew Paul taught that Jesus will forgive us for anything and everything. Paul told these people, "You say, 'I am allowed to do anything'—but not everything is good for you. And even though 'I am allowed to do anything,' I must not become a slave to anything" (1 Corinthians 6:12 NLT).

No one wants to be a slave—even to our screens.

. . . .

REALIZATION #3: More isn't always better.

. . . .

ASK YOURSELF OR A FRIEND

1. What is your favorite dessert?

2. When is a time you indulged in too much of a good thing? What happened?

3. Why do you think nine in ten teenagers see "too much time online" as a problem facing young people? Do you agree?

4. Why do you think almost 70 percent of teenagers wish they could spend more time socializing face-to-face than online? What's better about face-to-face?

5. Why does a follower of Jesus not want to become "enslaved to anything" even though Jesus will forgive us for anything and everything?

6. How do you know when screen time is becoming a problem?

7. What's one thing you can do this week to keep it from becoming a problem?

FINAL THOUGHTS

In 2018, just over ten years after the first iPhone was introduced, both Apple and Android software released updates including "screen limits."

Why?

The public demanded it. People began accusing tech companies of trying to addict us all to screens.

Funny, if you think about it. People demanded "boundaries."

Help us not look at our screens so much!

And so Apple's iOS and Android released updates with the ability to set screen limits, downtime, and other controls to help us not overindulge.

Our world is slowly realizing *less is more*.

I was a freshman in high school when I had my first boyfriend, and it was serious business. Sure, relationships then usually only lasted a month or two at best, but at fifteen, a month feels like a year. And to have a boyfriend on Valentine's Day, at fifteen, now that is a very big deal.

We'll call him Danny Romano instead of his real name (I dont' want to embarrass him). He was a junior, and he was Italian.

That's as romantic as it gets, folks!

He wasn't a model or anything, but at the time I was excited to get attention from anyone, especially a junior boy.

I met him at a church movie-party my older brother had at our house. "Met" is a relative term—I actually don't remember talking to him that night at all. In fact, I probably wouldn't have been able to point him out in a crowd if you had asked me at the end of the evening. But shortly after everyone had left the party, there was a ping on my pink Sony Ericsson phone, and I slid it open to see three attractive letters:

Hey.

I was completely breath taken.

My T9 texting skills improved rapidly over the next few days as I sent message after message to the mysterious junior boy from my youth group.

Alas, we finally met in person on Sunday at youth group and uttered but a few sentences to each other before we retreated back to the safety of our friend groups.

The next few weeks there were a couple of youth group hang-outs here and there and thousands of messages exchanged, and we slowly increased the number of sentences said to each other in person. Eventually he made his move and it was a done deal.

I was Danny Romano's girl.

February 13 rolled around, and we'd been "official" just a little over a month, so naturally things were pretty serious. (They were not.)

I had big expectations for my first Valentine's Day with a boyfriend. Would I get a bundle of roses? A box full of choco-lates? A giant stuffed animal large enough to catch the eye of every individual who walked by? The possibilities were endless.

Valentine's Day fell on a Sunday, so I knew we would see each other at church in front of all our youth group friends. And that is truly what Valentine's Day is about, flaunting your infatuation in front of everyone and their mother. (Unless, of course, the mother is your boyfriend's mother; obviously that would be highly inappropriate in this situation, but I digress....)

In my mind, everything was in favor of me having the best Valentine's Day ever.

I woke up and, like usual, my mom had set up a Valentine's gift for me outside my door while I was sleeping. There was a thick pink envelope with a tinfoil-wrapped See's Candies heart the size of my palm placed on top.

Awwww.

I smiled to myself. Any other year this would have been the most affectionate gift I received on Valentine's Day, but in my fifteen-year-old mind this was just an hors d'oeuvre for the epic Valentine's Day experience I was going to have.

I got ready, taking extra time and attention to get my makeup and hair just right. A girl has to look good for her first valentine, am I right? (Wrong. I was to learn in the next few years that boys don't notice the difference between five minutes of prep and fifty.)

I walked downstairs, passing my dad in the hallway, head buried in my phone.

"Good morning, Gorgeous," he said.

I don't even remember replying. This was typical. It was unconscious. I didn't mean to be ignoring everyone else, but I was.

Moments later it was time to leave for church. With a dreamy smile on my face, I slid into our family car, squished next to my brother, and closed the car door on the end of my jacket mindlessly.

Everyone in the car was talking, but I was busy typing on my phone. I was carrying on a conversation with three friends speculating what Danny might have planned.

We soon pulled up at church, and I knew the action was about to begin. I was sitting in the pews where the high schoolers usually sit when I saw Danny sneak in and sit behind me. I noticed he wasn't carrying anything. *He must have hidden my gift somewhere outside—wouldn't want to interrupt the service; that would be unholy.* The service ended and I slid over to him like a snake spotting a fresh egg.

"Morning, Danny. Happy Valentine's Day," I said in the sultriest voice I could manage. (In reality my voice sounded less like the Scarlett Johansson vibe I was going for and more like Rosie O'Donnell's version of Terk.)

"Hey," he said. "Morning. Valentine's Day, huh?" He began to look a little perplexed. "Happy Valentine's Day, ha-ha."

Good one, Danny. The old fake-out method.

Obviously he was joking with me. . .right?

I mean, I heard my mom say once or twice that boys are dumb, but I always assumed she was just referring to my brother.

We moved out to the foyer area with all the other youth and stole an appropriate amount of doughnut holes before slowly migrating into the Youth Room. Youth group started and ended and all the while I was waiting for the moment Danny would give me my Valentine's Day gift.

My standards started to lower over the course of that hour.
At first I was hoping, *Jewelry.*

Roses.

Stuffed bear.

That dissolved to, *Balloons. Small box of chocolates.*

Eventually I was thinking, *A single piece of candy!*

Youth group ended and there was no walking me out to his car, no jewelry, no roses, no stuffed bears, no balloons or chocolates or anything of the sort. Just a heart full of broken dreams and a junior boy, unaware that anything had gone wrong.

Distraught, I found my family and we got into the car. Bye, church. Bye, Danny Turd Romano. Bye, Valentine's Day hopes and dreams.

We got home and I sulked inside.

Food—that's what I needed.

I went to the kitchen to fix myself something (probably mac and cheese and tuna, because let's be honest, I couldn't make anything else), when I ran into a large bouquet of crimson roses on the kitchen counter with my name written in crude cursive on a tag attached.

I froze.

Slowly, I put both hands around the glass vase, looking at the perfect buds all bundled together. I had never received flowers before. It was the most beautiful and touching gift.

I opened the card to read the message. Honestly, to this day I don't quite remember what it said. Probably something cheesy like "To my little angel" or "Love you, Ditta [my nickname]. Happy Valentine's Day!"

But the message wasn't important; it was the name scrawled next to the dash.

Daddy.

Sometimes the people who love us the most are the people we ignored all day. I've never had a better Valentine's Day, and I never will.

REALIZATION #4: Sometimes the people who love us the most are the people we ignored all day.

ASK YOURSELF OR A FRIEND

1. What's the best gift you've ever received?

2. Why do you think Alyssa felt so disappointed in Danny?

3. What lesson did Alyssa learn?

4. Who are the people who love you the most?

5. How much attention are you giving the people who love you the most? How do your screens affect this?

FINAL THOUGHTS

It's funny—I don't really even know Danny anymore. I remember seeing him on Instagram. I think he had a girlfriend. (I wonder if he got her something on Valentine's Day!)

Frankly, I don't keep up with any of my high school boyfriends whom I spent countless hours texting, all the while ignoring my family. But here I am writing a book with my dad.

Two months ago was my birthday, and my mom and dad drove 440 miles down to visit me, take me to dinner, and then to breakfast the next morning. Then, while I was on an errand later that morning, my dad snuck into my office at work and left me balloons and flowers.

Why do I get the feeling that when I'm sixty-five, my ninety-year-old dad is gonna unhook his oxygen tank, sneak into my house, and leave me flowers?

Alyssa and I both love dogs. We've had a lot of dogs over the years. But I think we all have a special place in our heart for Jethro.

Jethro was our 105-pound Bernese Mountain Dog. Google-image one if you don't know what they look like. He was big, fluffy, and gorgeous.

Sadly, his life was way too short.

Five years.

That's all we got.

But those five years made a huge impact on our family.

Jethro was an impulse buy, a perfect example of why you should never take your kids to "just look" at puppies. Ashley, Alyssa's sister who was nine at the time, was obsessed with Bernese Mountain Dogs. I had never even heard of the breed, but she had bought books about them, stuffed animals, calendars. . .name it. Being adventurous parents (or stupid parents—you decide), we thought it would be fun to visit a breeder and "just look."

Yeah, right.

Next thing we knew, we brought home Jethro.

Jethro wasn't the most intelligent animal. He was big, klutzy, and nervous when he got in tight places. This was *not* a good combination when you happened to be walking through a doorway at the same time as Jethro. This dog was a knee injury waiting to happen.

Walking Jethro was always an experience as well. When my wife, Lori, took her first run with the dog, he ended up getting spooked, flanking her, knocking her to the ground, and giving her a scar on her knee that she still has today. He calmed down when he passed puppyhood, but he still outweighed each of our girls, which made him difficult to control if one of them wanted to go left when he wanted to go right.

He was a big boy!

Our family never owned a dog of great size before, so we never fathomed how much food this dog would consume. . .and eventually dispense from his body. We're talking serious dino doo-doo!

Add to this the fact that he always managed to wait for that perfect time to dump, usually during a walk. And not on the side of the road. Jethro would wait and squat in the middle of an intersection when we crossed a road. It's pretty embarrassing when your dog is building a miniature log cabin in the middle of a four-way stop while you're pulling out a two-gallon Ziploc for cleanup!

Despite these drawbacks, Jethro was always cheery with his tail wagging and a big goofy grin on his face. It didn't matter what kind of day you were having, Jethro wanted to be with you, snuggle up next to you, lay his monstrous head on your lap, and just love you.

And Jethro had what I would call a sixth sense. Jethro could tell when someone was stressed or anxious. If you were having a bad day, Jethro knew it. He could sense it in the same way dogs sense fear. It was almost as if Jethro had a sense of empathy. It was truly amazing. If you were worried, Jethro would calmly walk over to you, lay his giant head on your lap, and look up at you with his big eyes, as if to say, "It's okay. I'm here."

That's true empathy. Someone who doesn't try to solve your problems or give you unwanted advice like, "Here's what you should do. . . ." Empathy just says, "I'm so sorry that happened. I'm here for you."

Jethro was truly a comfort animal in every sense of the term.

When Jethro was about four years old, Ashley said something I'll never forget. She said, "I find Jethro inspiring!"

Rather than arguing with her, I simply asked, "What on earth is inspiring about this big doofus?"

"He's always happy," Ashley affirmed. "Even when times are hard, Jethro is content."

She continued, "There's no drama with Jethro. He doesn't hold grudges; he doesn't play favorites. He just loves you and wants to be with you, especially when you need it. Some friends come and go. Not Jethro. He's always there with a stupid smile on his big furry face. It's like he knows when I need a friend. He's inspiring."

I thought about these words from the mouth of a fourteen-year-old, and funny enough, I found that I could tolerate Jethro's shenanigans a little better after that day.

Unfortunately, Ashley was wrong about one thing.

Jethro wasn't always going to be here.

One rainy Monday while the kids were at school, it only took the vet about thirty seconds checking his lymph nodes for her to determine why he'd been breathing so heavily the last couple of weeks. Five-year-old Jethro had lymphoma.

"What does that mean?" we asked.

"It's a form of cancer. It basically means that he probably only has about thirty to sixty days left with you."

Thirty to sixty days.

It didn't seem real.

For the rest of the visit she told us about chemotherapy options that would cost as much as my car. These options wouldn't even heal him; they would actually make him very sick and might prolong his life just a few months. She didn't recommend this for Jethro. She simply said, "I'd just enjoy the time you have with him."

Sadly, we went home to tell the kids the bad news.

Thirty to sixty days.

Ashley took it the hardest, sobbing on and off for the next few days. Jethro had kind of been "her dog" all along; she was the reason we got him in the first place. But everyone was brokenhearted about the news.

"I hate knowing!" Ashley pronounced, tears streaming down her cheeks. "I wish I didn't even know!"

We sat and cried together on the family couch.

It wasn't long before Jethro wandered over, setting his big furry head on Ashley's lap. I guess she was right—he knew she needed him at that moment. Jethro was always there for you. He was the one with cancer, yet he seemed to be the happiest one in the room.

Ashley was right. The big furball was actually inspiring.

The dog was truly empathetic.

Empathy is an endangered species.

No, really. Empathy is rapidly becoming extinct among humans.

Empathy is the ability to "step into someone else's shoes" and feel what they're going through. An empathetic person isn't wrapped up in their own world. Instead, they notice someone else, seek to understand what they're going through, and cry with them.

But empathy is rapidly shrinking among our species as screen time increases.

A recent University of Michigan study revealed a 40 percent drop in empathy caused by the recent increase in screen time and social media use.[1] Screens are slowly bleeding out our ability to empathize, for two observable reasons:

1. People are so wrapped up in their own world—*Why don't I have more friends/followers? Why don't I have more*

likes?—that they aren't taking notice of others. (Could it be that 2 Timothy 3:2 predicted this?)

2. When screen time replaces true "face-to-face" time, we are literally becoming illiterate at reading the nonverbal cues and facial expressions of our friends. In other words, we don't know what "worried" or "anxious" looks like on our friend's face, and we sure can't read facial expression through text and emojis (more on this in a future chapter).

As a result, we are losing the ability to empathize in a time when depression and stress are at an unprecedented high and your friends need your empathy more than ever before.

How can you reverse this trend?

It starts with just putting your phone in your pocket when you're with someone else.

Simple, huh?

Try something when someone else is in the room. Put your phone away and look around. Consider the needs of others before your own (Philippians 2:3–4 talks more about this). Ask someone questions. Try reading their face. Get to how they are feeling. And when they talk, empathize. That is, mentally step into their shoes and try to feel what they're feeling. Don't give advice—just listen.

I warn you, if you do this. . .*you'll make lots of friends!*

Your friends will say things to you like, "Wow, you're a good listener." Or "You get me!"

It all begins with showing empathy. Taking notice. Just putting away your screen, looking your friend in the eye, and considering them.

REALIZATION #5: Empathy is the
gateway to deeper friendships.

ASK YOURSELF OR A FRIEND

1. What is the favorite pet you've ever had? Why did you like this pet so much?

2. How does Jonathan define empathy?

3. Why is it easier to empathize when you're face-to-face with someone?

4. Read Philippians 2:3–4. What advice do these two verses give?

5. Give an example of what "considering others" might actually look like.

6. What would considering others look like in your life this week?

FINAL THOUGHTS

Life those last thirty to sixty days with Jethro was a little different. He got a lot more table scraps. Who cares if they were bad for him!

Live it up, Jethro.

We walked him more, petted him more, hugged him more. We cherished every moment, thankful for the moments we got.

Exactly thirty days later, he was gone.

We miss you, Jethro. You were truly inspiring!

I drove to San Diego with a carload of friends recently. I'm not going to lie. It was horrible.

There's no better way to put it. It really was a bad trip.

I'm going to be brutally honest, because that's what everyone in my generation does anyway, right? Here it is:

- I spent way too much money.

- I swear we almost died on the road.

- I hated the way I looked all day. I felt so ugly.

- I got into a fight with one of my best friends.

- I felt like no matter how hard I tried, I didn't belong.

All these feelings led me to do something dramatic. You're going to laugh, but once you hear my story, hopefully you'll realize it's not such a crazy idea.

I am taking a break from social media.

For a year.

Yeah, that's right. *An entire year!*

You might think I've lost my marbles, I know. But really this is the clearest I have thought in a long time.

Let me back up a little bit.

It was a Saturday morning and I was looking forward to going to this event near San Diego with my friends. We were going to a fun beach volleyball event on one of the most gorgeous Southern California beaches, wearing matching outfits, and then after the event we were going to get some food and hang around the area.

Should be great, right?

Nope.

Not even close.

All five of us piled in the car in matching tank tops and Converse, our delicious lattes from our local Santa Barbara coffee shop in our hands. The event location was about three hours away, and I somehow secured shotgun. We were listening to fun music, bopping along and laughing with each other.

So far, so good.

But then it began.

Just a little bit at first.

It started when the driver pulled out her phone every once in a while to check a message or notification. Sure, a lot of people have done this, me included, but come on. . .*this is never okay*. And every time she'd do it, the car would start veering to one side or another, sometimes literally into another lane (which is a good reason you should never text and drive).

At first I didn't say anything. Besides, I have pulled out my phone real quick while driving too. I'm not going to pretend like I'm immune to the temptation. And I didn't want to give her grief for something I had probably done with her in the car before too.

But she did it again. . .and again.

I finally looked over to see what she was looking at. She had Instagram open.

Okay, really?

It wasn't like she was typing an emergency text (not that any typing is smart while driving).

Then she began looking for something on her map.

"I can look it up for you if you want," I offered.

"It's fine, I got it," she snapped at me, obviously irritated that I was encroaching. She probably felt judged, and I get that. I get defensive when I feel like I'm being watched too. But four other lives were at stake, maybe more if you consider other vehicles.

We got to the event, and the mood lightened. We were laughing and dancing around to the music blasting on the beach, playing beach volleyball. I'm using the word *playing* loosely. Most of us were terrible. But the more we messed up, the more we laughed.

But there it was again.

Phones out constantly.

The focus more on *recording* the event than *enjoying* the event.

As the event drew to a close, I turned to say something to my friends, but they were buried in their phones.

All of them.

They were posting the videos and pictures they had taken.

I looked at my phone. I had only taken one video, and it wasn't even a good one because I was bouncing around laughing while I shot it.

Eventually we wandered toward a trendy beach path with grass and palm trees that was truly "Insta-perfect" and began taking pics. I joined in, posing in a couple of group pictures and deciding I was going to pose silly so I didn't look like I was trying too hard.

These pics are gonna be great.

They weren't.

As I looked at all the images on my tiny screen, zooming in to see which one was best, I didn't like any of them.

Are my arms really that big? They didn't look that fat in the mirror this morning. Why do I look like Jabba the Hutt all of a sudden?

Plus, everyone else looked really good in the pics.

I couldn't help but compare.

That's one thing Instagram always does to me. It makes me compare. **And comparison is the thief of joy.**

I put my phone down. I didn't care. *Whatever—I had fun dancing, right?* That's what it was really about. Ignore the bad photos of Jabba Alyssa. *Alyssa the Hutt!*

I tried to ignore the nasty voice in my head telling me that the other girls looked way better than me in the shirts we all wore together. I knew this wasn't a voice I wanted to listen to.

But everywhere we went. . .

"Let's take a quick pic!"

Again.

And again.

And again.

The rest of the day I tried to pretend like I was having fun, but I felt like a square peg trying to fit in a round hole. I was awkward and not as stylish as my friends. My tank top looked blah, I hadn't posed well enough for the photos, and maybe I should have documented the event better.

As I look back at these thoughts, I now realize how shallow and stupid my thinking was, but at the moment I was stuck in a spiral of corrosive thoughts and I couldn't escape them.

On the way home I fought with my friend again. I started nagging her about looking at her phone, she snapped at me, and I snapped back. It was a mess (grumpy Alyssa doesn't always make the wisest choices).

The drive home became very quiet.

I directed my gaze toward the side window, excluding myself from any of the conversation. As I gazed out at the ocean along the Pacific Coast Highway, I didn't even notice the beautiful landscapes, the small beach towns cozied up to the serene waters. All I could see was my fat arms poking out of the ugly tank top I couldn't wait to get out of when I got home.

When we finally got back to Santa Barbara and they dropped me off, I bolted inside my house expressionless only to plop on my bed and pull out my phone. I had several notifications from Instagram. Probably letting me know I was tagged in those horrible photos we took earlier. I opened the app to check, but the notifications were not from photos I was tagged in. In fact, I looked at all my friends' stories and realized I wasn't in a single photo!

I started to cry.

I literally wept like the five-year-old child who didn't get the toy she wanted for Christmas.

I dropped my phone on the floor, closed my eyes, and fell asleep.

Hours later I woke up in a cloud of despair. I didn't even know why. Maybe it was the fight. Maybe it was because no one tagged me. Maybe it was because those pics made me feel like I was packing on the pounds. It was most likely all of these things.

All these elements had one common factor.

Instagram.

Don't get me wrong. I'm not saying Instagram is bad. I've had some good times with the app. You probably have too. But one thing was very clear: our day had been hijacked by Instagram. We had allowed it to take us to unhealthy places.

Why did social media have such a hold on me?

Honestly. If my friends and I had all left our phones at home (which I never would have done; how would we even get to San

> **INTERESTING FACT:**
>
> Researchers have debated about the effects of social media for years, but they finally agreed on two things:
>
> 1. There really is a mental health crisis engulfing adolescents, particularly girls, in all major English-speaking countries.
>
> 2. The link between social media use and the mental health of young girls is strong and consistent, and in the vast majority of experiments where girls reduced their use of social media, mental health improved.*

Diego in the first place—a paper map?), I would not have been feeling so miserable and dejected.

I needed to do something, but I didn't know exactly what. I just knew I needed a break. **I needed a break from all this pressure I was feeling.**

So I did it. I didn't even have to think twice. I took out my phone and deleted the Instagram app.

In fact, I researched and discovered there was a way to remove your Instagram account and have your pics disappear off everyone's devices the next time they refreshed.

Gone in an instant.

In seconds, my account was gone. Completely vanished.

Immediate relief swept through my veins.

Insta-gratification.

I didn't know how long I was going to do it at this point; I just knew I needed a break.

A few days later, I told my dad what I had done as we were talking on the phone. I was doubting myself.

"I think I'm gonna take six months off."

"I'm proud of you, baby," he told me, audibly chewing something (yes, McKees are always eating). "A break might be nice. It doesn't mean you have to do it forever. But give yourself some time. A lot of people find it refreshing."

"I don't know," I said, thinking out loud. "It's so dramatic."

"Don't feel sucked into the drama. If you need a break, then take a break."

"I don't know," I said honestly.

"I don't think you'll really miss it." *chomp chomp* "You can do it."

I admired his belief in me, and his ability to eat tacos so late at night without getting indigestion, but I brushed his words off, thinking my six-month break would be impossible, not to mention an overreaction!

But the more I thought about it, the more I was appalled at

myself for doubting myself.

This could be a really good thing!

The Irish stubbornness that runs through my veins came to the surface, and somehow I decided I was going to double the six months and take a whole year off.

A whole year!

Yes. I decided it then and there.

Why? Because I am beautiful. And I want to have fun at events and not see myself as *Jabba Alyssa* for the rest of the day because I don't know how to take pictures properly. (Really, I'm the worst at posing for pictures!) And because I love my friends, and I didn't want to fight with them because of Instagram.

One year from October 2019.

I was taking a break.

· ·

REALIZATION #6: When social media begins hijacking our lives, it's probably time for a break.

· ·

ASK YOURSELF OR A FRIEND

1. Name a time you were trying to have fun with friends but screens "hijacked" the moment.

2. Have you ever taken a media break or "fast" before? How was it?

3. How can breaks like this be helpful?

4. How do you know when you've reached the point where screens are becoming a serious problem in your life?

5. What is the longest span of time you think you could go without social media?

6. How do you think your friends would react if you went

"off the radar" in social media? Does it really matter what they think?

FINAL THOUGHTS

I thought I was good at monitoring my social media usage, and for the most part I was pretty good at it. But sometimes even a little bit can be too much.

It's good to monitor yourself, to make sure you're practicing healthy habits and sometimes challenging yourself and stretching yourself so you can become a better person.

I challenge you. Can you take a break from Instagram? How about a week? How about a month? How about a year?

I promise you this: I support you 100 percent if you decide to try it. I am going to do something really vulnerable here. Here is my email: TheAlyssaMcKee@gmail.com. I'm not joking. Email me your name and why you have decided to take a yearlong social media fast, and I will pray for you the same day I receive that message. I don't guarantee a reply, because hopefully I am being present in the moment. But I will check those emails at night and pray for you specifically before I go to sleep.

You're not alone! In fact, I bet one of your friends or family members might do it with you, or at least hold you accountable to do it.

I quote my dad: "I don't think you'll really miss it." *chomp chomp* "You can do it."

(Is anyone else hungry for a taco right now?)

Go for it.

Dare to be different!

"Thanks for speaking to us today."

Hundreds of kids were filing out of the gym headed to their next class. This particular girl made a special effort to come talk with me after the assembly. I had just spoken to them about being screen-wise.

"Thanks for the encouragement," I replied. "Was it any help?"

"Yeah," she said, and turned to walk away, but paused for a second. "Especially the part about sending pics." Her eyes teared up. "Thank you." She scurried out the door.

It happens at every school I speak at.

Literally every one!

I come to speak, and the principal, a teacher, or a kid tells me the story of a girl in the school who sent a pic to some guy only to regret it.

Like Emily.

Emily had only been dating Tyler about a month when he first asked her to send him a nude. Emily didn't feel comfortable with her own body and wasn't really excited about sending naked pictures of herself, so she tried to avoid the conversation. But Tyler really began to put on the pressure.

"Come on. What's the big deal? Sending nudes is a simple commodity of love these days."

Emily wasn't buying it. *Tyler doesn't even know what the word* commodity *means.*

Tyler kept pressing.

"Who cares? Just use Snapchat. It will disappear."

"You'll just screenshot it!" Emily said.

"No, I won't," Tyler promised. "I'll just peek really quick."

This went on for weeks. Finally, one night after staying up late messaging each other in the dark, Emily gave in, Snapping him a vulnerable pic of herself. (Not a lot of wise decisions are made at one in the morning.)

At least it will disappear, she told herself as she sent it.

A little notification immediately appeared on the screen.

TBSwag05 took a screenshot.

Emily messaged him back.

"You promised!"

"I'm just kidding! I'll delete it."

"Do you promise?"

"I promise."

A month later, when the two of them broke up, Emily discovered that his promises never amounted to anything. **Of course, she didn't know until she noticed people snickering and looking at her funny in the hallways.**

It wasn't long until her best friend Abby pulled her aside.

"Did you see it?" Abby asked.

"See what?" Emily said.

Abby gulped. She didn't even respond; she just pulled out her phone and showed Emily a large group text about what a "ho" Emily was. . .with a picture attached. . .the picture Emily had hoped Tyler deleted a month prior.

Emily didn't finish school that day; in fact, she didn't even finish the year. She couldn't stand the comments and stares, so she switched schools completely.

Emily isn't alone.

I've met plenty who've experienced the same thing. Sometimes the story ends with a suicide attempt. The results are never pretty.

Every school I visit has had a similar occurrence. At one school I visited, a freshman guy was convinced by three older girls to send them a nude video of himself. They promised reciprocation (you send it to us, we'll send one to you). As soon as he sent it, they forwarded the video to the whole school. As a result, the school literally shut down for a day because every kid in every classroom was laughing and talking about it—no one was focusing on school.

Allow me to quickly mention that I'm actually choosing *not* to talk about something obvious here. I'm not going to talk about the many problems with sending nudes, taking nude photos of yourself, or looking at nude photos (which is actually prosecutable in many states). All these aren't wise moves and aren't going to help you in your future romantic relationships at all (and I spend an entire chapter talking about these issues in one of my previous books, *The Teen's Guide to Social Media and Mobile Devices*). That being said, right now I want to focus on another very important topic: *regret*.

In all of these situations, people experience regret. Both the person who sent the pic and the incredibly mean person who decided to send that pic to other people—yes, most often, even that person feels regret.

Regret is kind of an interesting feeling. It's a mix of guilt and shame a person feels when things didn't turn out the way they hoped. Regret almost always is combined with feelings of *I wish I would have known. . .*

Think about that for a second.

If only I would have known. . .

Guess what? *You know.*

Yes, just by reading this chapter and listening to the experience of others, now you know these three simple truths:

1. Pics that were supposed to disappear typically reappear.

Don't ever post anything you wouldn't want the whole world to see. Nothing is private once you hit SEND.

2. People can be incredibly mean. Guys and girls alike. Even the people closest to you.

3. It's never okay to post mean pics or comments about someone, no matter how much you think they deserve it.

Sadly, many people don't think before they hit SEND, so these truths are often learned the hard way.

But you don't have to learn truth the hard way. The simple fact that you have this book in your hands right now reveals that you are open to learning wisdom, seeing danger, and steering clear of consequences.

The Bible calls this being "prudent."

> The prudent see danger and take refuge, but the
> simple keep going and pay the penalty.
> (Proverbs 22:3 NIV)

The prudent person realizes there are lessons to be learned whenever we see people experience this kind of pain. Wisdom observes and adapts. You can learn from the mistakes of others and steer clear of many of these hardships.

REALIZATION #7: Disappearing posts tend to reappear.

ASK YOURSELF OR A FRIEND

1. Have you ever regretted something you posted? What happened?

2. How do you feel about what Emily's boyfriend did—putting pressure on her and then showing the pic to the whole school?

3. Is there anything Emily could have done to avoid what she experienced?

4. How can we "take refuge" from this kind of danger?

5. What are some of the "penalties" people pay when they don't think before they post?

FINAL THOUGHTS

It doesn't matter where this situation happens; three different groups are always represented, and they always respond the same way in the end.

Group 1 is the person who sends a pic and eventually regrets it. They always say the same thing: "That was supposed to be private!" or "I didn't know he/she was going to do that."

Group 2 is the person who decides to send this private picture to other people, an action that is beyond mean. It's cruel and vindictive, and in some states it is actually a felony if the picture is of a person under eighteen, because then it is considered distributing child pornography. In some cases it turns out to be manslaughter—when the person in the picture takes their own life. Just like if you were texting and driving and accidentally ran over a sweet little ol' lady. It doesn't matter that you didn't mean to—your actions caused a death.

Group 3 is the group of bystanders who end up bearing witness to it all. And if they decide to laugh or show the picture to others, they immediately become part of Group 2.

Whenever I talk with someone in Group 2 or 3 after the incident occurred, they always say the same thing. "I didn't think it was such a big deal," or "If only I would have known. . ."

Guess what?

Now you know.

In all of these situations everyone experienced pain and regret.

In all of these situations everyone wished they could just hit REWIND and do things differently from the beginning now that they saw how the story ended.

You know how the story ends.

You can change the story before it even begins.

I have a confession.

It's one I have always been very embarrassed of and kept secret for most of my life because it makes me sick to my stomach when I think about it. But in the self-practice of bringing things into the light rather than hiding them in the darkness, I have tried to talk about it more the last few years. Because here's the thing—and I'm sure you've heard this before, but it needs to be taken to heart—the truth will set you free. And if I'm being honest, I used to lie a lot. Lying was my thing. I actually became a really good liar.

If I'm real with myself, I think this had a lot to do with the fact that I am a people pleaser. Ever since I was a little girl, I always hated when others were mad at me or didn't approve. My parents would barely raise their voices and I would burst into tears.

I remember when I was in second grade and I said something mean to one of my classmates. My classmate then proceeded to run and tell our teacher, Mr. Peterson, that I had called her a name (tattletale).

Poor Mr. Peterson, a young teacher probably fresh out of school, had to get on his knees and tell me to "pull a card" because I had misbehaved. Pulling a card meant walking up to the front of the classroom and retrieving a red card from a slot by the whiteboard. It was like a ref giving you a red card in soccer for bad behavior. Little did my teacher know what would come next.

I started bawling!

Big ugly tears poured down my snotty face and immobilized me in my seat. I wouldn't stop crying and eventually he tried to console me, patting me on the back and telling me that it was okay and I didn't actually need to pull a card (not the best discipline tactic on his part, but I applaud him for the effort).

Aside from my need to people-please, there were other reasons I was so skilled at lying. I was a good liar because my brother was a really bad one. I quite literally learned from his mistakes. And my dad was like a detective. I swear, he was a master at knowing when we kids were up to no good.

I remember when we were small and my dad asked my brother if he had flossed his teeth before he went to bed. Just a typical parent kind of question, right? My brother stumbled over his words, turned bright red, and avoided eye contact.

"Y–y–yesss," he said with a shaky voice, obviously lying.

My dad looked at him with a raised eyebrow and paused. "Okay then. Show me the piece of floss from the trash."

My dad followed him into the bathroom and watched as my brother went over to the empty trash can, hoping a piece of floss would magically materialize in the trash on the journey across the tile floor.

Not a strand to be found.

My father was not pleased. But I keenly observed from afar, making mental notes to always think three steps ahead. If I ever skipped flossing my teeth, I always made sure to throw a piece of floss in the trash just in case he checked. And if my mom or dad were to quiz me on whether or not I had flossed, I knew I had to look them directly in the eye, confidently, in order for them to believe me. (Or with all that effort, perhaps I should have just flossed my teeth.)

By my senior year of high school, I was a master at lying.

It was no longer pieces of unused floss in the trash, but instead the occasional leaving class early for "yearbook assignments" or "going to the bathroom" to meet some boy down the school hall for a mid-class smooch (once those braces came off, there was no stopping me). And beyond class time, I was beginning to bend the truth with friends too, telling them confidently that I had seen an R-rated movie I surely never would have been allowed to see. Or when I told my classmates that I couldn't meet for our small group project on a Wednesday night because I had to watch my sister, when in reality, I didn't want to tell them I went to youth group at church on Wednesday nights.

And then my lies leaked into my social media.

My Instagram page was full of happy-looking photos with inspiring "love yourself" captions.

Lies.

In reality, I was so insecure and ashamed of my "fat" arms that I cropped them out of photos and decided to eat only salads for a week straight.

I went off to college and the pattern continued from small white lies to larger ones. I told my roommates that I had dated a current Navy SEAL, when really, I had just kissed a boy who was now an enlisted soldier.

The lies flowed so easily now. I told my mom I was going to church, when in reality I hadn't been for weeks. When my younger sister, Ashley, came to visit, I told her the rude girls who had sat on my bed in my dorm room weren't really my friends but were just girls who came into my room sometimes. But at the time, they were the closest friends I had.

I was ashamed.

I so desperately wanted people to like me that I was pretending to be someone completely different. **Social media made that easy. It's easy to edit who we really are on social media.**

But I didn't like who I really was. I wanted people to think I was a "good person," a "happy person," when in reality I was miserable and drowning in my own lies.

I didn't know how badly I needed help.

My lies began catching up with me at the end of my second year in college. My boyfriend and I started fighting nonstop. I became clingy in fear of losing him, and soon, this guy who looked so in love with me in all the Insta photos we posted together didn't even want to spend time with me. I don't blame him. I was not being the person I was meant to be.

I began hanging out with very bad influences. If I had met these closest college friends years before, I would have been shocked.

I began sneaking around the Resident Director in charge of my college dorm. We snuck guys in our room past curfew, as well as a few bottles of alcohol. And while this might be the usual for some college students, it was dramatically different from the girl I was pretending to be to my parents back home. I was living a double life, and it was tearing me apart.

One day my roommates and I got into a huge fight and they began ignoring me. Like literally pretending I did not exist. They trashed some of my personal items I had left in our common space, and I started to feel unsafe in my own apartment.

Then my boyfriend and I got into one of the biggest fights we had ever had. He said he needed space—as in, I can't handle you right now—and I felt completely alone and hopeless. I had no one to turn to. I felt like no one would care if I existed anymore.

So I decided I was going to numb the pain.

I didn't think twice about it, alone in my room that afternoon, as I drained a pill container of Tylenol down my throat. It was all I had in my medicine drawer. I slipped into bed and closed my eyes.

Ten minutes later I shot up abruptly in my bed. What had I just done?

This was not what I really wanted.

I gagged myself, throwing up as much as I could into the toilet. I rested my head on the porcelain and sobbed. What would my family think if they could see me now? I was so ashamed.

I crawled back into bed and tried to go to sleep, hoping I would be okay, ashamed at what I had done and not wanting anyone to know.

I woke up twenty minutes later and felt sick to my stomach. The ceiling was spinning as I tried to sit up in my bed, unable to hold myself up. I panicked and immediately realized I didn't want to live like this anymore.

I called my mom, and for the first time in a long time, I told her exactly what I had done that day.

She was awesome.

My dad was across the country speaking somewhere, so my mom immediately booked a flight down to my college in Southern California, then called my boyfriend directly and told him to drive me to the emergency room.

In the next forty-eight hours I had to answer a thousand questions from doctors, telling them what happened, why I was overdosing, and most importantly, that I didn't want to die. I wanted to live!

I wasn't telling lies anymore. As scary and life-altering as that was going to be, I told the truth. My family knew. My boyfriend knew. All these random doctors knew. There was no hiding it. My life was a mess, *but I wanted to live.*

I can't even begin to describe the feeling. It was like a giant weight had lifted off me despite the rough roads I knew were ahead. There was something comforting about just being real and getting the help I needed.

No more lies.

That was about five years ago as I sit here and write this with tears in my eyes thinking back on all that happened. And I can't believe all God has done for me in the last five years.

No, I'm not perfect, I've had my moments (ask my sister), but God has completely changed me.

First, He gave me a fresh start. I confessed all my garbage to God, to my family, and to the few good friends I had left, and they accepted me as I was, mess and all. I know I was fortunate to have people in my life who were willing to do that—some of us don't. But even if you don't, God is willing to take you as you are regardless of your mess-ups. Paul says that as plain as day in his first letter to Timothy:

> This is a trustworthy saying, and everyone should accept it: "Christ Jesus came into the world to save sinners"—and I am the worst of them all. (1 Timothy 1:15 NLT)

God doesn't hold your past against you. He is truly an architect of new beginnings. He definitely was for me.

Second, God helped me change my surroundings. I had surrounded myself with some pretty bad influences, and I needed a change. Turning away from those bad influences required surrounding myself with some good influences who would warn me if I began believing lies again. . .which is exactly what this verse is talking about:

> Be careful then, dear brothers and sisters. Make sure that your own hearts are not evil and unbelieving, turning you away from the living God. You must warn each other every day, while it is still "today," so that none of you will be deceived by sin and hardened against God. (Hebrews 3:12–13 NLT)

God doesn't want you to try to make a fresh start on your own. He wants you to guard your heart, and a good way to do that is by hanging out with friends who will encourage you and help you stay connected to truth.

That's exactly what I did.

I transferred to the amazing college where I now work, got plugged into a local church, and began hanging out with people who encouraged me to live an authentic life.

Authentic!

That was something new for me. And what a relief to not have to live in hiding anymore.

Third, God gave me opportunities to get involved serving others. As He changed me and I began to grow in my own faith, I started volunteering at my church, helping young people who were experiencing some of the same struggles I had faced. And that's what's interesting—I've learned I'm not alone.

I can't tell you how many people I've encountered who felt exactly like me.

I'm not good enough.

People wouldn't like me if they knew everything about me.

If only I were skinnier, prettier, had better skin. . .

I've met so many people who are hiding behind the mask of perfectly posed pics or cleverly crafted comments, or who are simply isolating themselves, hiding behind a screen.

Guess what?

I see you.

I really do.

I was there.

You don't need to hide anymore. You can experience a fresh start.

. . . .

REALIZATION #8: Many of us think we're safer
hiding behind our masks, but it's only a
matter of time before we're exposed.

. . . .

ASK YOURSELF OR A FRIEND

1. Why do you think Alyssa began lying?

2. What do you think Alyssa was afraid her friends would

think of her if she told the truth?

3. Do you ever find yourself worrying what other people think of you?

4. Do you think most people post authentic glimpses into their lives on social media? Explain.

5. What did Alyssa feel once she confessed the truth to her parents, her boyfriend, and the doctors? Why did she feel this way?

6. What do you think the verse from Hebrews is encouraging us to warn each other about?

7. Is there someone you need to talk to so you can get real about your life? Who? How about right now?

FINAL THOUGHTS

I wish I could tell you that I never feel bad about myself anymore.

I wish I could tell you that I never worry what others think.

I wish I could tell you that life is simple.

It's not, but now I have Someone with me on this journey, Someone who knows everything about me and loves me anyway. I'm not talking about a boyfriend or even my parents. I'm talking about God.

I'm being honest (yeah, I'm trying to do that now), this was a tough chapter to write. So I'm going to close in a prayer to God, praying the same thing King David prayed in a handful of verses of Psalm 139. You can pray this with me if you want:

O LORD, you have examined my heart
    and know everything about me.
You know when I sit down or stand up.
You know my thoughts even when I'm far away.
You see me when I travel
    and when I rest at home.

You know everything I do.
You know what I am going to say
     even before I say it, Lord.
You go before me and follow me.
You place your hand of blessing on my head.
Such knowledge is too wonderful for me,
     too great for me to understand! . . .

You made all the delicate, inner parts of my body
     and knit me together in my mother's womb.
Thank you for making me so wonderfully complex!
Your workmanship is marvelous—how well I know it.
(Psalm 139:1–6, 13–14 NLT)

And in my own words I pray, "God, thanks for loving me enough to give me a fresh start, forgiving me of my past, and giving me a new beginning. Give me the strength to walk in Your way each and every day, living an authentic life the way You designed."

Amen.

My phone is probably my favorite tool. . .besides my chainsaw.

Okay, I know, that probably sounds a bit redneck, but I have put over one hundred hours on my chainsaw this year.

Two years ago our family bought some property, two houses on three acres. It's fun because we have two generations pitching in and living on the same property, each with their own house, sharing a nice yard, a pool, a big garden, and three acres for the dog to explore. My wife, Lori, and I are in one house, my parents are in the second house. . .and there's plenty of room when Alyssa and her brother and sister come home for the holidays (which then turns into three generations on one property).

These particular three acres proved to be a lot more work than we anticipated, especially because the people who owned the property before us didn't do jack squat with it! The whole property was overgrown with countless dead trees and rambling vegetation everywhere. Simply put, one of the first purchases we made was a chainsaw.

I had never used a chainsaw before, but they sure looked fun! Chainsaws are so powerful. I couldn't wait to start cutting through logs like butter! (Is it just me, or do guys like to destroy things?)

But luckily the salesman who sold me the chainsaw warned me.

"Have you ever used one of these before?"

"Never," I replied honestly.

"Well then, let's take a few minutes to talk about this powerful piece of machinery so you don't cut your leg off."

I laughed, because I thought he was exaggerating.

But he didn't laugh. (Don't you hate that? Awkward.)

Then he began telling me stories, all true stories, of guys in the neighborhood who tried to use their new chainsaw and ended up dead, or in the hospital if they were lucky.

He had a friend who was just cutting wood in his own backyard for the winter (a lot of people cut wood for their wood-burning stoves around here) when he slipped on some pine needles. In the split second it took him to release his finger from the chainsaw's trigger, the chain ripped through the inside of his leg near the top of his thigh.

"Do you know about how long it takes you to bleed out when you slice open your femoral artery?" he asked.

I shook my head.

"A good slice with this saw to your upper thigh and you can bleed out in less than a minute!" he said, demonstrating with the saw as he talked. "And depending on how many acres you have, most of the time, no one will ever hear you. You'll just lie there in a pool of your own blood."

I went home and told Lori all of his stories. Honestly, they kind of freaked me out. I was a little scared to run the saw by myself.

"He's not kidding," Lori said. "You slice your femoral artery out on our property. . .you're done!"

Now Lori was freaking me out!

Lori worked in surgery when we were first married. She was a surgical tech, the person who passed the surgeon instruments. She was also the one to whom they handed body parts after cutting them off. She had done several amputations, including mangled legs.

"They're heavy," she explained.

"What?" I asked.

"Human legs. They always hand me the leg after they cut it off!"

"*Ewwww!*"

So before I ever turned on my chainsaw, I went down and bought some chaps. They are basically thick pant legs you wear when you're using your chainsaw. If you slip and the chain hits your leg, the chaps get all caught up in the blade and basically stall the saw before it can cut into your leg.

I've cut down almost fifty trees with that saw and cut the logs into firewood (and given away a bunch of it to my neighbors—more wood than I could ever burn myself).

That saw has been by far the most effective tool on our property.

I love my saw, but I'm aware of its danger.

That's the way it is with many of the powerful tools we use. We need to be humble enough to recognize, *Hey, this thing can be dangerous. I'm gonna use a little caution.*

I can't help but think of this proverb:

> The wise are cautious and avoid danger; fools plunge ahead with reckless confidence. (Proverbs 14:16 NLT)

Sadly, I've witnessed far too many people "plunge ahead with reckless confidence," ignoring the power—and yes, even danger—their phone yields.

A phone is a very effective tool. It makes my job soooo much easier. My job is basically getting on a plane, landing in some other city, getting into a rental car, and driving to wherever I speak that week. My phone is my GPS, my boarding pass, my car rental confirmation, my hotel room key (yes, my phone literally opens the door), and most importantly—it's my connection to my family back home!

I remember the days when I used to have to print out boarding passes, car confirmations, maps, directions, phone numbers, correspondence. . .I had a stack of papers I brought with me on every trip.

Now I just bring my phone.

My phone does everything.

But even though my phone is extremely helpful, *I recognize its danger.*

Much like a chainsaw, my phone is a powerful little device. A phone can be used for good or bad. I can use it to help me with all this travel, or I can allow it to hurt myself and the people around me. You see, my phone is a great tool when it's used correctly. And just like my chainsaw, it can mess me up if I misuse it or underestimate its power.

We now live in a world where the majority of people spend more time staring at screens than interacting with their spouse or children.

Think about that for a second. A husband spends more time looking at a TV screen than hanging out with his wife. A woman spends more time scrolling through her social media feed than being with her husband.

Screens can be helpful tools, but they become dangerous when they distract us from connecting with the people we love.

For example, a recent study revealed "excessive device usage decreased marital satisfaction."[1] You probably don't need a psychologist to tell you that when two people spend increasingly less time together because they're buried in their screens, *the relationship suffers.* Studies also show that screens and social media create conflict and can make couples dissatisfied in their relationship.[2]

Screens can actually kill a marriage.

Divorce attorney James J. Sexton told *Newsweek* that social media is a prime factor behind broken relationships. "I can't remember the last time I had a case where social media was not either a root cause or implicated in some way. And it's always the same story: people maintaining affairs via social media or communicating with people they don't have any business communicating with. Infidelity is so easy now, and it's poisoning marriages."[3]

That's pretty scary.

Phones are powerful. Be careful not to underestimate their danger.

- -

> **REALIZATION #9:** People underestimate how dangerous screens can become when they distract us from the people we care about.

- -

ASK YOURSELF OR A FRIEND

1. What is your favorite part of your phone?

2. In the proverb Jonathan shared, what word is used for those who "plunge ahead with reckless confidence"?

3. What are some areas where people "plunge ahead with reckless confidence" with their screens, ignoring dangers?

4. Are there any areas where your use of screens has tempted you to flirt with danger?

5. How can you effectively "be cautious and avoid danger"?

FINAL THOUGHTS

My wife, Lori, and I both enjoy the convenience our phones provide, but we're also very aware of the dangers a phone can pose. No, it won't saw your leg off, but sometimes it distracts you from what's important. . .like the person sitting right next to you.

I've personally known countless couples whose marriage faltered or ended because of screens.

That's scary.

Like chop-off-your-leg scary.

I like my phone, but not better than my wife and kids!

Do you ever engage in small talk?

You know, extremely shallow conversation when you bump into someone you don't know very well and you don't know what to say?

"Great weather today, huh?"

"Yeah. Love that sun!"

"Yessiree!" (*Awkward pause*) "Very warm."

"Indeed."

"Yes indeedy."

(*Another awkward pause*)

"Well, nice seeing you!"

Who talks like that?

No one wants to, that's for sure.

Sadly, we won't engage in deep conversations if we don't have deep relationships.

This was my dilemma. I had lots of surface-y friends, but I lacked deep relationships. I was feeling the symptoms of this problem but didn't really understand the root cause until I sat down and talked with someone who really knew me—my grandpa. I call him Papa.

Papa and I have a unique relationship, one that I wish more granddaughters had with their grandpa. Every time I'm in my hometown, I always make sure I sit down and have coffee with him. He truly is one of the most intentional people I know, and

I love catching up with him over bear claws and other delicious carbs. He is my mentor, my friend, and, I'm lucky enough to say, my biggest supporter. When I'm struggling, I always look to him for advice first (you'll hear more about him in future chapters).

Every time I sit down with him, he asks me questions *about me*. Not just surface stuff like, "How's work?" But deep questions about who I am and what I'm feeling.

So as we sat down at Panera this particular time, he began asking me about me, specifically my relationships. It wasn't long before I was sharing my frustrations—my lack of close, deep relationships with my peers currently surrounding me. Why was it that I had so many people around me but still felt so lonely at times?

Papa reassured me, "I know you're feeling lonely right now, but Alyssa, I know that anyone who has had the chance to really know you like I do can't help but really love and appreciate you."

I bashfully accepted this compliment and continued to visit with him, brushing the comment off as something any grandfather would say to his grandchild. But later that night I thought more about what he had said to me.

"*. . .anyone who has had the chance to really know you. . .*"

I started to wonder.

Do any of my friends really know me?

Have I given them the chance?

Then it hit me. *How can I expect people to open up to me if I don't show them that I really care to know who they are?*

This is the Golden Rule plain and simple: "Do to others whatever you would like them to do to you" (Matthew 7:12 NLT). It's all through the Bible actually. Paul said it pretty simply in his letter to the Philippians: "Let everyone see that you are considerate in all you do" (Philippians 4:5 NLT).

It's amazing how this simple, foundational truth can change your interpersonal relationships.

I gave it a shot. I figured the best way to be considerate of others was to emulate my papa. I asked questions. Not just any questions, but deeper, more intentional questions.

The next time I was with one of my roommates, I looked her in the eye and began asking her "second-level" questions. I didn't ask her the typical, "How was work?" or "When did you get those new Lululemon shorts? They're super cute!" (They were.) Instead, I asked questions that required more attention and genuine consideration. I call these second-level questions because they're not the kind of questions you ask people you have just met. You ask them when you're ready to move to the second level of a relationship. Questions like. . .

- "Do you see yourself here in this same run-down beach house in five years?"

- "What is one thing you wish more people knew about who you really are?"

- "Would you ever consider adopting a kid?"

And even though some of these might be yes or no questions, they can't be fully answered in just one word. They require thought and emotional response.

How do I know?

Because whenever I ask someone a question like this, the first thing they do is put their phone down.

Yeah. Really.

Try it. Ask:

- "What's the best thing that someone has done for you this year?"

- "Who is someone you really look up to? Why?"

- "If you could go back and redo one day of your life, what would you change?"

You'll know it's a second-level question if they put their phone down.

Second-level questions go deeper. Not uncomfortable deep, but "I care" deep.

Second-level questions provoke people to share.

Second-level questions encourage eye contact.

Second-level questions cultivate communication.

Second-level questions get people to put their phone in their pocket.

I started trying this gradually with my friends. Sometimes I would practice on my sister to see if my questions were too odd and out of the blue. (If you're reading this, Ashley, I'm sorry I used you as my guinea pig.) But little by little I learned more about the friends around me. As I started to show more intentionality in my relationships, my friends opened up more and even began to reciprocate this intentionality toward me. They didn't always reciprocate, and that's okay. But most of them did, happy that someone was making an effort to notice them.

I asked about them; they asked about me.

Like last week. I was sitting on our stained couch, looking at my phone, when one of my favorite roommates walked in the door, smiled, sat down next to me, and asked me a second-level question. . .*and I put my phone down.*

Can you ask a question that makes someone put their phone down?

REALIZATION #10: Second-level questions motivate people to put their phone away.

ASK YOURSELF OR A FRIEND

1. Who is someone you feel safe talking with? Why do you think they make you feel safe?

2. Who is someone who feels safe talking with you?

3. Who is someone you wish you could talk with more? What would you like to talk about?

4. What are a couple of second-level questions you could ask them?

5. How can you engage this person with second-level questions this week?

FINAL THOUGHTS

I can't even count the number of times I wanted to tell a friend, "Hey, do you mind putting your phone away while we're sitting here talking?"

But I never did.

It probably would have come across as rude, although no more rude than they were being by looking at their phone instead of paying attention to me.

But now I have a way of getting my friend to put their phone away without me having to say, "Hey, can you put that stupid thing away?"

I just ask them, "Hey, if you could text anyone in the world and you knew they'd text you back, who would you text?"

Questions like that provoke people to put their phone down. Then I follow up that question with ones like these:

- "What would you text them?"

- "What would you hope they replied?"

- "Who do you text more than anyone else?"

- "Who do you wish would text you more?"

- "What do you wish they knew about you?"

- "What's keeping you from telling them?"

What questions can you ask that will prompt your friends and family to put their phones down?

Bored, a little jet-lagged, and killing time at the airport before boarding her flight to Cape Town, Justine Sacco tweeted a few attempts at humor.

"Weird German Dude: You're in First Class. It's 2014. Get some deodorant."

"Bad teeth. Back in London."

Funny? Maybe. It didn't seem to matter. It's not like she had a massive following.

Before takeoff, she posted one final tweet to her 170 followers.

"Going to Africa. Hope I don't get AIDS. Just kidding. I'm white!"

Sacco didn't think anything of it as she switched her phone to airplane mode and faded off to sleep. But eleven hours later when she landed and connected again, her phone blew up with hate messages, including one from her manager informing her she had been fired.[1]

True story. One retweet led to another, and by the time Justine Sacco landed at Cape Town International Airport, tens of thousands of angry tweets had been sent.

Sacco's account was deleted, but her tweet lives forever.

Her life was never the same.

Many of us have never considered exactly how much our choices affect our ability to get—or even keep—a job. Social media has only inflated this reality, because now there's a written record of almost everything we say and do.

I interviewed several employers while researching this book, asking them how much social media impacts who they hire and fire.

"I love social media," one office manager told me candidly. "Whenever someone turns in their application to me, the first thing I do is pull up their social media accounts and scroll through them for a few minutes. **Seventy percent of the time I'll throw away their application based on something they posted.**"

Social media has transformed work environments and completely changed the way most employers hire and fire. Today employers frequently use people's vlogs and social media posts to check up on them.

My friend "Allison," a human resources consultant, encounters this frequently. "Human resources" is the department in any large corporation that handles the hiring and firing. If you are accused of saying something insensitive at work, you have to go see someone from human resources.

I asked Allison how much social media had affected her job, and she told me countless stories of people being fired because of something they posted on social media. For example, one of her companies had an employee who worked from home and sent in a time card clocking exactly how many hours she spent working each day. This young woman was a vlogger, posting videos about her life throughout the day. One day, she posted a video saying, "I don't feel like working today...," and took her online audience on a shopping adventure. This time-stamped video was during a time she claimed she was working. Little did she know her boss was one of her followers. She was terminated immediately.

"Most of these young employees forget how easy it is for their boss to access their personal social media," my friend Allison said. "After all, the majority of young people allow anyone to follow them, hoping to increase their number of followers. Maybe they should realize that their boss might be one of those followers."

Allison also explained that anything employees say after hours on a digital platform can still be considered harassment. She consulted for a company who had an employee who would pop on Facebook each night and rant about the company and other employees. They fired this guy for harassment and damaging the reputation of the company.

"My job has almost become easier," Allison admitted. "Social media provides documentation of almost everything now. All we have to do is pull up screenshots of what they said on their Instagram and they're out of a job."

Defamation claims (suing someone for insulting or slandering) used to be "he said" or "she said," but now there's a written record. Everything you post has potential liability, especially if you want to move up in your career. The higher you get, the more closely you're watched.

Even if you don't have a job yet, remember, nothing you post is temporary. One small comment, one pic you send to a friend—you never know when and where those will show up or who will see them. . .*like the college you want to attend.*

A recent survey revealed that 31 percent of college admissions officers said they had visited an applicant's social media page to learn more about them. If you are careless about what you post on social media, some colleges definitely weigh that into consideration. Like Harvard, for example, when they actually revoked admission to ten incoming students who participated in posting offensive memes and images "mocking sexual assault, the Holocaust and the deaths of children, sometimes directing jokes at specific ethnic or racial groups."[2]

Freedom of speech? Sure. Harvard freed them to go to some other school.

Again, seems pretty obvious. Our posts can radically affect

our future. But here's where I'm going to give you some advice different than what the world might give you. The world would say, "Be careful what you post!"

I'd like to take it a step further.

Be careful how you live.

If you're living right and treating others right, then you're posting right. But if you live wrong and treat others wrong, then you constantly need to think about what you post so you don't get caught living wrong!

And consider this: if you call yourself a Christian, then you are using the name of Christ to describe yourself. That should make you think hard about how you live.

Do others see Christ in your actions and words?

After all, the Bible tells us, "Whatever you do or say, do it as a representative of the Lord Jesus, giving thanks through him to God the Father" (Colossians 3:17 NLT).

Does your life represent Jesus?

Does your social media reflect Jesus?

. . . .

REALIZATION #11: Your posts affect your future *faaaar* more than you realize.

. . . .

ASK YOURSELF OR A FRIEND

1. If you could have any job in the world, what would you want to do?

2. Where do you think you'll work five years from now? Ten years from now?

3. How can someone live in a way that represents Jesus— what does that look like?

4. Who do you represent?

5. What is something you've seen someone post that probably could come back and haunt them later?

6. How can you be more careful about what you post?

FINAL THOUGHTS

Most employers are beginning to use social media to screen potential employees and get a realistic picture of the kind of lives these individuals live. Five minutes on someone's Instagram account can tell them a lot.

What does your Instagram account tell others about you?

What could your future schools or bosses find on your social media?

What would you like them to see?

My coworkers are the coolest!

No, really, I've never had such cool coworkers in my entire short life as I do in my current job! But I don't think I ever realized it until we put our phones away during lunch.

Our entire lunch!

LUNCH BREAK

My coworkers are such a strange mix of different personalities; it's a wonder we get along so well. One of my coworkers likes to point this out to us all the time, as if we are a major anomaly to be such good friends despite our differences. But it really isn't that surprising if you think about it. We are all around the same age and were all hired because we are good communicators. Face-to-face conversation has never been hard for any of us. . .which keeps things interesting during our lunch breaks.

Earlier in the book I mentioned I work in the admissions department of a Christian college in Santa Barbara. It's a cool place to work, and we've gotten in the habit of eating together for our lunch breaks, usually in the "dining commons," where the college serves meals.

We all fill up our trays and sit down to eat, all the while swapping stories of the crazy interactions we had with people that day, or talking about the cool cities we'll visit to meet prospective students.

"I'm headed to Chicago next week!"

"Lucky! Make sure you eat at Portillo's!"

Eventually all our food is gone, and we still have about half an hour before our lunch break is officially over. Some of us pull out our phones, and some of us continue to swap stories. This is the way it always goes.

Unless. . .

Unless we go to Chick-fil-A.

No, I'm not being paid to sponsor them, although I gladly would. But I am about to talk about how glorious Chick-fil-A is, because it is absolutely the best place ever to have a lunch break. And no, not just because their chicken is fantastic. The reason I love Chick-fil-A so much is because of all the hilarious moments my coworkers and I have had when we've taken our lunch breaks there.

All thanks to the "Cell Phone Coop."

Have you ever heard of the Cell Phone Coop?

I didn't know about it at first, but when I went to our local Chick-fil-A with my coworkers the first time, they showed me how it worked. When you arrive and place your order (mine is always a spicy chicken deluxe meal and at least three sauces, because go big or go home), you also pick up a Cell Phone Coop. Once you open the little carboard box decorated like a chicken coop, you place the phones of everyone from the table into the little coop and close it up. Make sure your phone is on silent, because you don't want to be the reason everyone loses out if the phone goes off and you have to pull it out of the box.

And that's just it—you can't take it out of the box the whole meal!

If you succeed, you can exchange the coop for a free ice cream cone. One for each phone in the box.

Yes, *free ice cream*! I haven't seen this promotion at every Chick-fil-A, but I'm sure glad mine offers it!

You can see now why I am so enamored with Chick-fil-A.

(And yes, not much is better than ice cream in my opinion. The McKees highly enjoy food and sweets.)

But I have to admit, the free ice cream isn't all we gain from our phone-free lunches.

The best part is the smiles.

It didn't take me long to notice. **When the phones are locked up, the smiles emerge shortly.**

I can't quite pinpoint it. Something about taking a break from the office and giving our *whole and complete attention* to each other gets the most ridiculous conversations going. Our banter is always fun, and the smiles always break to the surface no matter the topic. We could sit forever debating the stupidest subjects back and forth.

One of my colleagues, Andy, gets a kick out of asking controversial questions. He does it just to stir the pot. He probably couldn't care less about what he asks, but he purposely plays devil's advocate and tries to defend the least popular opinion. We know he can't be serious, but the 7 percent inside of me that thinks he might be drives me absolutely insane and I just have to fight back.

Then there's Miles. Miles is the most happy-go-lucky guy you will ever meet. And he is irritatingly good at everything he does. But he's so kind and cheerful you can't actually get mad at him ever.

Once, when we finally turned in our Cell Phone Coop to get our ice cream, Miles decided he needed to try to flip his ice cream cone. We were all laughing hysterically, confused on why and also yelling at him not to do it as he smiled ear to ear and bobbed his hand up and down, ready to flip at any moment. He tossed his cone in the air, and it seemed to flip in slow motion. Then the cone returned perfectly to his hand and froze flawlessly in place.

We cheered, erupting in laughter, going back and forth,

betting each other that we couldn't do it better. I flipped my cone confidently and watched it soar in front of me, bounce off my wrist, and hit the red plastic tray in front of me.

All laughs.

All smiles.

People from other tables were looking over at us trying to figure out what all the fuss was about. They were probably curious why a bunch of twentysomethings were being so loud, laughing and having fun in the middle of the day with no screens to be seen. Because you just don't see that anymore.

We were all ice cream flips and smiles, drips of vanilla running down our wrists shamelessly. Because when you're on your lunch break with all your friends at Chick-fil-A, there's no reason to have your phone out.

Maybe you don't live near a Chick-fil-A or don't have the Cell Phone Coop. No worries. Just throw your phones in the center of the table facedown and make a deal: first person who touches their phone during the meal buys dessert for everyone. You'll find the uninterrupted face-to-face conversation much more rewarding.

Think about it. Do you ever really *need* your phone during lunch with friends?

· ·

REALIZATION #12: Meals are always better without screens.

· ·

ASK YOURSELF OR A FRIEND

1. Name a few friends you'd love to have lunch with.

2. Describe a time when you ate with a friend and they were more interested in their phone than you. How did that make you feel?

3. During meals, what is the typical phone etiquette (manners) for you and your friends—checking phones constantly, only checking if it's important, or keeping phones tucked away completely?

4. How would you like your current phone etiquette to be different? Why?

5. Why do you think Alyssa and her friends have more fun when they put away their phones during lunch?

6. Are any barriers or hesitations preventing you from suggesting something like this with your friends? How can you overcome those barriers?

7. What is a way you could change up your phone etiquette during meals this week?

FINAL THOUGHTS

It's not like I never use my phone—in fact, my coworkers and I use phones frequently for work and for social fun. But we've discovered that mealtime is a sacred time where we have the most fun when we put our phones away.

Totally away!

When we do. . .the laughter always erupts.

So when are you going to try it?

(*Where's your nearest Chick-fil-A?*)

CHAPTER 13
Power Outage

Ever been home when the power went out?

Kinda freaky at first. Everyone's running around the house looking for flashlights or candles. Someone always runs outside to check the electrical panel just in case the breakers tripped (which is crazy, because *all* the breakers never trip at once. . .but someone still checks the panel).

Once the realization hits that power is gone, a sense of adventure kicks in!

This is what a zombie apocalypse would be like!

Silence.

Darkness.

At first people will use their devices. But if the power outage is long enough, even devices run out of power.

Then what?

It's funny, but something interesting happens in times like this.

Families talk.

Like more than normal.

I'm thinking about all this because I'm actually writing with the power out right now. We've been experiencing high winds and lost power yesterday. We're hoping it will come back on soon.

Here I am, in the dark, typing on battery power, racing against time (can I finish a chapter or two before the battery runs dry?).

But honestly, I don't mind too much when we lose power.

Lionel (my perpetually happy Labrador mix) and I just walked outside before sunset to get a few chores done. We stopped by the woodshed so I could grab a stack of oak and a handful of kindling to build a fire.

An hour later, with Lionel curled up on his little bed in the corner of the room, I built a fire, more for light than for heat. It's our typical power-out activity. My wife, Lori, and I always snuggle together in front of the fire, usually with a book, while Lionel snores in the corner. (Yes, he really does snore. Pretty adorable.)

When the kids were home (they're all twentysomething and out on their own now), they always seemed to love the adventure aspect of power outages. Maybe that's because whenever the power went out, we made it fun!

"Power's out! We're grilling tonight!"

No power means no electric oven, so we'd throw something on the grill outside, then bring it in and eat in the light of the flickering fire.

After dinner it was game time. And by games I don't mean *Call of Duty* or even Monopoly. Usually I pulled out some game idea my kids had never heard of, like Silent Animal Circle, a competition where everyone wants to be the elephant. (So fun...now my kids still want to play it even though they're adults! Message me if you want to know how to play.)

If the power was still out before bed, I'd wrap up the night with a classic scary story, the kind I usually would tell around the campfire camping. And if I ran out of stories, I just made one up on the spot.

Here's the thing: **for some reason, when the power was out, we almost always had a better time than when the power was on.**

Don't get me wrong—our family has had some really fun memories with screens! (McKee movie night was a regular Friday night activity.) I'm just saying, it was always all smiles when the power was out.

Whodathunkit!

Screens are fun, but so is an occasional break from screens.

As it turns out, my kids aren't alone.

Last year a group of researchers embarked on a fascinating study of teenagers who weren't able to access their phones or social media for a few weeks.

Yes, weeks!

The study followed young people at a camp with no Wi-Fi, no cell service, and no devices. Instead, the teenagers had to just hang out with each other and interact face-to-face.

Guess what happened?

They loved it.

They preferred it.

And I don't think you'll find that I'm exaggerating. In fact, 92 percent of the teenagers experienced "gladness" and admitted it was "beneficial to have gone without their phones while at camp."[1]

It's not that they don't enjoy their phones in everyday situations; they just realized that their phones would have taken away from their camping experience. In fact, when asked, "they almost unanimously admitted they would have spent the entire time on their phones."[2]

What these teens and my own kids each experienced is what experts are calling "tech-free zones." And many mental health advocates like myself recommend seeking out these tech-free zones every once in a while to give yourself a break from screens.

Who knows? Maybe you'd like it. Maybe you'd be in the 92 percent who were glad to take a break.

How about just twenty-four hours?

How will you know if you never try it?

• •

REALIZATION #13: *Occasional tech-free days are surprisingly refreshing.*

ASK YOURSELF OR A FRIEND

1. What did you do last time your power went out?

2. If your power went out for three days and all your batteries ran out in the first day, which screen would you miss the most?

3. What would you do those two days with no screens?

4. Why do you think a bunch of teenagers hanging out together with no screens were glad not to have screens?

5. If you had to try going tech-free for a few days this month, how could you make it fun—or at least bearable?

6. What friends would be fun to ask to go tech-free with you for a few days?

FINAL THOUGHTS

The teenagers at the camp in the study above discovered something else very surprising. They discovered, and I quote, "face-to-face communication is far superior to screen communication when it comes to building friendships and getting to know other people."[3] In fact, one camper even commented that she got to know her camp friends better in just a few weeks than her friends she had known for years back home.

Hmm.

A few weeks of face-to-face, real-life communication brought her closer to others than she'd felt before.

When are you gonna try it?

Welcome to the chapter I didn't want to write.

Why didn't I want to?

Because the topic makes me uncomfortable. It will probably make you uncomfortable too. And ironically, that's exactly why I'm writing a chapter about porn.

Porn is one of the readily available vices on our screens that hurts face-to-face relationships, and almost no one is talking about it. . .*which is exactly what I want to talk about.*

Yes, you read that correctly. I'm actually *not* going to do what you might expect and list out all the things wrong with porn or try to scare you away from it. (I can't help but think of the PE teacher in the movie *Mean Girls* who is teaching sex education and says, "Don't have sex, because you will get pregnant and die!") It's not that I don't believe porn is harmful; I believe it's incredibly harmful. It's a huge distraction from healthy, real-life intimacy, and many people become entangled in it and struggle to break free. In fact, I encourage you to take a peek at the countless studies on the subject. My dad's book *Sex Matters* is really helpful and dedicates an entire chapter to escaping porn.

But that's not what I want to talk about.

I want to talk about *talking about it*.

Allow me to explain.

Growing up, I rarely heard about pornography. I grew up in the church, hanging out with my friends at youth group all through middle school and high school. And while my dad and mom did a great job helping me understand sex and intimacy, I still didn't hear about porn very much.

Dad admits this. He says he wishes he had talked with us more about the reality of porn, the probability of stumbling upon it, and the importance of understanding what it is so we'd know how to respond. If he had a do-over, he'd talk more about it. And if I had a do-over, I'd be way more open with my friends about it.

But I didn't hear much about it at all. I just knew it was bad. . ."*so don't do it!*"

That was fine and dandy, but just because we know something is harmful doesn't mean we can simply stop—problem solved. We know too much sugar is bad for us, but that doesn't mean we are immune to the temptation. Have you seen the checkout line at Trader Joe's? It's a trap to get you to buy sugar at the end of your healthy grocery shopping spree.

Even though I wasn't particularly interested in porn, it was kind of a mystery to me. Super awkward. That thing we don't talk about.

I heard that guys typically view it more than girls, and that it was something we shouldn't look at, because that would be lusting. . .and lusting was bad. But that was pretty much the extent of my knowledge. Plus, honestly, it just wasn't much of a temptation for me.

So I didn't talk about it.

My parents didn't talk about it.

My church didn't talk about it—well, not really.

Here's how it was when I was in youth group. Once a year they'd separate the guys from the girls. The female youth leaders would take all of us girls into one room and tell us about modesty, letting us know that it wasn't our bodies that defined our worth and that we deserved to be viewed as more than objects. Then they would tell us we were beautiful children of God. We would come back to the youth room glowing and confident, feeling beautiful and affirmed.

I'm not knocking it. Really. It's a good message to communicate to young ladies, especially when their screens are sending opposite messages of "Dance like this, dress like this, act like this. . .because guys will like it." Sexualization 101. *Sigh.*

But little did we know that all the while, the male youth leaders were talking to the guys about pornography. They were giving them all the facts, statistics, and scripture, getting down to the nitty-gritty truth of the matter. And admittedly, now I understand a little bit why they focused the porn conversation on the guys. Recent studies show that 72 percent of young guys seek out porn regularly, where only 36 percent of young girls do. Interestingly enough, even 41 percent of committed Christian guys seek out porn regularly, and 13 percent of Christian girls.[1]

Why not talk with the girls about it too?

I mean, if you have thirty young girls in your church, and all of them are committed Christians, then statistically four of them still "seek out" porn regularly. And then again statistically, about half of the girls will be dating guys who are "seeking out" porn regularly (check my math; it's spot-on).

But we never talked about it.

Imagine my shock when I first heard my boyfriend tell me he had viewed pornography while we were dating. I was confused.

But why?

~~He's a nice Christian boy.~~

Nice Christian boys don't look at pornography, do they?

Wrong.

And boyfriend after boyfriend, I slowly began to realize it was much more common to look at pornography than I thought—nice Christian boy or not.

I was distraught. How could they do this to me? It meant they were desiring other women. Plus, porn was so disrespectful to women. I was tortured by the thoughts in my head of my boyfriend thinking about other women.

Then I began actually comparing myself to these unknown women my boyfriends were looking at, and I started thinking irrationally.

Am I not sexy enough?

Am I not "going far enough" with him?

I don't want to do those things that the girls do in pornography, but does that mean he won't like me?

Maybe I need to be more like the girls in those videos, but that would be wrong—right?

These were my honest unfiltered thoughts. I was so confused. (And yes, it's a little embarrassing to write them out. But I'm hoping my honesty will help you if you ever encounter thoughts like this.)

Looking back, I've realized something. While I was so distraught with these thoughts, emotions, and feelings, I never even considered the difficulty my boyfriends had with the effects of porn. I wasn't compassionate or understanding about the very real temptations out there and how difficult it was for them to avoid those temptations. I was stuck in my own insecurities, embarrassed and not wanting to talk about it. And I definitely didn't assure my boyfriends at the time that they could talk to me and their friends about their struggles with the temptation. They felt just as embarrassed and confused—not to mention ashamed.

And none of them were talking with anyone about it. This was embarrassing stuff. It's tough to talk about.

"Hey, Chris, have you been sneaking your phone out at night and looking at porn? I have."

It's not something we talk about.

Think about that for a second.

Porn is a huge struggle affecting over half of young people today, but we don't talk about it. Sadly, most of the people who do talk about it are the people who joke that it's no big deal, ignoring the real-life consequences.

Most of my friends never talked about it. They felt awkward. They felt judged. My boyfriends felt judged by me, so they swept it under the rug and avoided talking about it again.

Here's the problem: **if you sweep it under the rug. . .it's still there!**

So what are we supposed to do?

I'll tell you what we're supposed to do. We're supposed to talk about it. And I can prove it using a scripture that most people ignore.

Seriously. Many of you have already read this verse, and if you're like me, you missed the second part. Everyone ignores the second part, but it's the part that will actually help you and me.

Check it out. It's an easy scripture to remember because it has a bunch of twos. It's 2 Timothy 2:22, and I want you to pay specific attention to the second part:

> Run from anything that stimulates youthful lusts. Instead, pursue righteous living, faithfulness, love, and peace. Enjoy the companionship of those who call on the Lord with pure hearts. (2 Timothy 2:22 NLT)

So many people talk about the first part of this verse but ignore the second. Look carefully, because the secret to doing the first part is in the second.

I've heard numerous sermons on "running away from lust." And during every one of those sermons I thought, *Okay. Sure. But how? Have you tried to watch Netflix lately? Have you ever been on YouTube? Sexual imagery is all around us. And even if I don't struggle with the temptation, my boyfriend does! So please tell me: How are we supposed to run away from lust?*

The key is in surrounding yourself with others who are following the Lord. In fact, when we surround ourselves with good influences, we're empowered to pursue what's right and actually run away from lust. Friends can help us put together a game plan to avoid becoming entangled in porn.

So who are you surrounding yourself with?

Are you encouraging each other to pursue what's right?

Are you talking about these tough issues with each other?

I didn't.

I wish I did.

- -

REALIZATION #14: The best way to escape temptation on our screens is to talk with someone honestly about our struggles. . .no matter how uncomfortable.

- -

ASK YOURSELF OR A FRIEND

1. Have you ever talked with someone honestly about pornography?

2. Is it a hard topic for you to talk about? Why?

3. Who is someone you feel safe talking to about difficulties in your life?

4. What does 2 Timothy 2:22 tell you to do with anything that stimulates lust? How can you do that?

5. Why do you think a verse about fleeing lust advises us to surround ourselves with godly people?

6. Name three people in your life with whom you'll work toward being more open and understanding.

FINAL THOUGHTS

Years later, I had an amazing boyfriend who was very vulnerable with me and told me about his struggle with a pornography addiction. He had heard it was bad, yet he had turned to pornography at the end of the day because it was easier to escape in it than to talk through his problems.

Eventually he met a friend who also had struggled heavily with pornography, and this guy shared about his struggles with my boyfriend, asking for support. My boyfriend at the time then felt like he could open up with this guy about his struggles and count him as a safe person to talk with for support and accountability as he tried to run away from temptation and get out of his bad habit.

I was shocked to hear about the struggles my boyfriend had dealt with, but I didn't want to scare him away from talking about them and realized that he had trusted me enough to tell me about his struggle in the first place.

I took a deep breath, kissed him on the cheek, and told him I was there for him and was thankful he trusted me enough to talk about it. I told him I wanted to support him and that I hoped he knew he could always tell me if he struggled with porn again and I would be there for him even if he slipped up.

He was taken aback. No girlfriend had ever reacted this way, and he felt grateful to have my support and care.

Better late than never, right?

Do you ever wonder how emojis came to be?

Because people were tired of their texts being misinterpreted.

It's true. Emojis are just a feeble attempt to provide facial expression so texting is a little more understandable.

Think about it. You text your friend a question:

Do you want to come over and hang out?

Three little dots emerge.

You wait.

Eventually, one word appears.

Sure.

Most of us can't help but wonder. *What does she mean by this one-word reply?* The possibilities abound. She could mean...

A. For sure! Woo-hoo! There's nothing I'd rather do! That sounds awesome!

B. Sure. Hanging with a friend sounds okay.

C. Sure, and I really do want to, but I'm extremely busy right now and have no time to type out a long reply!

D. Sure, I guess. I mean, I have nothing else to do, so I'll settle for hanging out with you. Sigh.

Which of these did she mean? (*Please be choice A.*)

We don't have a clue because we can't hear her voice or see

her face. How are we supposed to know what "sure" really means?

Funny, sometimes people will jump to conclusions and get all upset over what a text "could have meant" when really it didn't mean that at all.

Did she mean choice D? Rude! That's so typical of her. I don't know why I even asked her.

Then you receive a text.

Sorry for my short response. I was at the hospital visiting my grandma. She just had surgery, but she's okay now. I'm really looking forward to hanging with you tonight!

Gulp!

This typical miscommunication in digital messages existed long before texting. Email and every kind of instant messaging suffered the same shortcomings. Why?

We can't see what are called "nonverbal cues." And nonverbal cues are exactly what the words imply, little cues or hints as to what the person is saying through nonverbal channels like facial expression, volume, and tone of voice.

Think of the last time you were severely upset and someone asked you, "Hey, how are you doing?"

You might yell sarcastically, "Oh, I'm just great!"

The words of your reply don't match your nonverbal cues, but anyone within fifty feet of you knows loud and clear that you meant, "I'm doing anything but great! Leave me alone!" But that's not what you said verbally. It was your tone, volume, and other nonverbal cues that made it clear.

My friend Karla received a text from her grandma when a close family member had died. Grandma typed some sympathetic words, then ended with LOL! Karla wondered when Grandma had turned into such an evil ice queen, laughing at Karla's misery. Turns out, Grandma thought LOL meant "lots of love."

That's the problem with texting. Soooo prone to misinterpretation.

Don't get me wrong. I love texting. Texting has its place. If you want to ask someone, "What pages do we have to read in our science book tonight?" then texting is very helpful. Or "What time should I pick you up?" Great method of communication.

But let's say you text your friend, Hey, how are you feeling? Let's be honest. You have no idea what they mean when they text you back, Fine.

In fact, a bunch of researchers tested communication effectiveness a few years ago in a clever bonding experiment where they tested pairs of close friends for "emotional connectedness" as they engaged in four different types of conversations:[1]

1. In person

2. Video chat

3. Phone call

4. Text messaging/instant message

The results were fascinating.

The researchers measured the bonding in each situation through the level of understanding the friends reached and the level of emotional connectedness they experienced. Interestingly enough, the participants felt connected in all the communication situations, but the measured bonding differed "significantly" for each one.

Guess which communication method made participants feel "most connected."

The "in person" method won by a landslide.

Why? Because when people were face-to-face, they could not only hear what the other person was saying but also see their gestures and facial expressions, and sometimes even reach out and touch the other person—giving a hug, for example. In-person communication was by far the most rewarding to participants.

Video chat was second best, because facial expressions could still be seen. Nonverbal cues are a huge part of communication, but a video chat still isn't as good as being face-to-face. Most of us experienced this when we were forced to stay home during the COVID-19 lockdowns. Even though we could FaceTime our friends, it still wasn't as rewarding as truly connecting with them in person.

Phone was third in the experiment. People didn't feel very connected just talking on the phone. But tone and volume were still perceivable. Participants could pick up sarcasm and voice inflection.

Texting or instant messaging was dead last, simply because it was prone to the most misinterpretation. All caps, exclamation points, and emojis try to fill in the gaps, but it just isn't the same as verbal, nonverbal, and face-to-face communication.

Does this mean you shouldn't text?

Not at all.

But you might think twice about engaging in important conversations via text or instant message.

How many times have we said it in this book?

Face-to-face is better!

· ·

REALIZATION #15: Texting is prone to misinterpretation.

· ·

ASK YOURSELF OR A FRIEND

1. If you had a choice to be face-to-face with a friend or texting them, which would you choose?

2. Why do you think some people feel more comfortable communicating through screens?

3. Can you think of a time when you misunderstood someone's text or they misunderstood yours? What happened?

4. When is texting the most convenient?

5. When is a time you think face-to-face is better?

FINAL THOUGHTS

I think I'll text Alyssa to test this theory of texting.

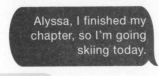

Alyssa, I finished my chapter, so I'm going skiing today.

Shut up!

There it is again! What does she mean?

A. Shut up, as in, that is so cool! You're so lucky!

B. Shut up! I don't want to hear it. I still have to write a chapter today. I hope you fall and break your leg.

I should have just called her and left a voice message!

CHAPTER 16
I Wish My Family Did That

Nielsen research has been tracking TV watching since 1949...because people love watching TV.

The average American household has the television on over seven hours a day.[1] More during national catastrophes. In fact, many families just leave it on during dinner.

My house was a little different. Don't get me wrong—we enjoyed watching TV and movies together, but nothing got in the way of family dinner.

Especially on taco night!

Yes, I guess we probably looked a little like those families in old movies who sit down and eat whatever Mom has lovingly prepared. Dad would even typically ask us, "Okay, everyone share their high and low of the day." We'd go around the circle and share our best and worst moments of the day. We were one of the few families I knew who still did this, but that didn't bother me. I actually loved it.

For one, my mom is a really good cook. She makes all sorts of different dishes, and for the life of me I still can never replicate the way she makes them. But also, I always really did enjoy catching up with everyone at the dinner table. Sometimes this was one of the few times someone actually truly listened to me share my thoughts and feelings, especially in the midst of my middle school years. Let's be real. Middle school friends don't typically say, "Alyssa, how are you feeling? You look stressed."

So I never rebelled against the idea of family dinners growing up. . .until eighth grade. Because in eighth grade I got a phone.

Everything changed.

I was no longer a carefree child interested in the daily life of my family. Who cared if my sister had a bad day? I had supercool junior high friends, and I texted them every chance I had.

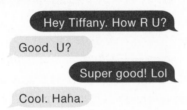

Hey Tiffany. How R U?

Good. U?

Super good! Lol

Cool. Haha.

I know, stimulating. And I wasn't about to let dinnertime interfere with these vital conversations. So whenever I felt my pocket vibrate, I'd slyly whip out my phone under the table and return a text. I didn't see a problem with that. Who cares if my brother is sharing about how excited he was to play some new video game?

Eat.

Buzzzz.

Text.

Eat.

Ignore my family.

Buzzzz.

Text some more.

This phase was short lived. Dad quickly noticed the constant clicking of my thumbs (we used thumbs on our old-school T9 phones), so he made a new rule: No tech at the table.

I was outraged.

I had a life! I had friends. I had skinny jeans and black hoop earrings from Claire's. Dinner was interfering with my priorities. "No tech at the table" was devastating. How was I supposed to reply to my middle school boyfriend the second he sent me a text?

But "no tech at the table" led to many fun conversations and great insights I would have missed if my little pink phone screen was there. Yes, it might have taken some diligent prodding from my parents to start us talking, figurative and literal. No, really, my mom tickles very aggressively—her fingers are like little daggers! Yet somehow we came around and started laughing and talking together.

I never knew this was weird—laughing and talking together. But apparently it was. How do I know? Because we constantly had friends over for dinner and all of them would comment, "You guys eat dinner together? Wow."

Take my friend Megan, for example. The first time she came over was my junior year of high school on taco night. Taco night is a big event at our house. Usually at least three or four of us are in the kitchen preparing. Dad was always making his special bean mixture and one of us kids was chopping lettuce and tomatoes. So when Megan came over, we immediately put her to work.

My dad immediately showed her how to make his epic bean mixture (one part black beans, two parts refried, Cholula, garlic salt, and waaaay too much medium cheddar), while Mom cooked the meat and I chopped jalapeños.

I looked over at Megan. My dad had her stirring the pot of beans while he asked her countless questions like, "So what position are you playing in soccer now? Is that your favorite position? Why? Do you still want to play soccer when you go to college? What colleges are you looking at?" I rolled my eyes, because he was always doing this. But she didn't mind. **She was just a little surprised someone was taking an interest in her life, because in her experience, most adults didn't.**

Welcome to my house, Megan.

When everything was ready, we sat down, prayed together, and ate. Dad immediately asked, "Okay, everyone: your high and low of the day," and we each shared. When it was Megan's turn, she said, "My low was when my sister borrowed my sweater without asking, and my high. . .*this dinner*!"

I thought she was just being polite, but later that night when we were doing homework, just the two of us, she asked me, "Do you guys *always* eat dinner together like that?"

"Yeah. Most nights."

"Wow." Megan pondered that for a moment. "That is so cool. I wish my family did that. We don't talk. Everyone just watches TV while eating something on their own."

I'll never forget that.

"I wish my family did that."

I guess I never realized how good we had it.

Sure, **research actually shows** that kids who engage in regular family dinners. . .

- are 40 percent likelier to get better grades in school.

- are 30 percent less likely to engage in disordered eating.

- are two and a half times less likely to use drugs.

- are two times less likely to use alcohol.

- have fewer emotional and behavioral problems.[2]

But that's not what Megan noticed. Megan just enjoyed our fun and meaningful face-to-face conversation.

And honestly, I did too.

No tech at the table. . .maybe it wasn't such a bad thing after all.

REALIZATION #16: Dinner is better with the people at the table, not the ones in your palm.

ASK YOURSELF OR A FRIEND

1. When was the last time you were at dinner with someone and they were on their phone the whole time? Were you irritated? (Duh.)

2. Let's be real—have you ever done the same thing?

3. What is one way to keep from looking at your phone during a meal with someone?

4. Why do you think people feel the need to be on their phones when they're sitting across from someone?

5. What is one goal you can make for yourself to promote conversation at mealtimes?

FINAL THOUGHTS

It's funny how dinner conversations I had over ten years ago can still be so crystal clear in my mind today. Some of my most prominent childhood memories happened around the dinner table. And you know why that is? My parents took a deliberate interest in us, showing us that we were important enough to pay attention to and teaching us what was important—intentional conversation with those you care about. (Maybe that's why those kids in the study who engage in regular family dinners on average tend to make better life decisions.)

Thank you, Mom and Dad, for being so purposeful about conversation around the table. You taught me to prioritize the people in front of me by leading by example, and I am so grateful.

I know I will do the same with my kids someday. Because face-to-face conversations matter.

I remember when my kids first asked me for a phone.

"All my friends have one. Plus, it will help me connect with you better!"

That sounded reasonable. And it made sense. Phones are effective communication devices, so shouldn't they help us connect with others?

Well. . .do they?

I guess that's the big question: Do phones help us connect with others?

Think about it. **Phones might be a great tool for connecting with people outside the room, but only if they don't interfere with your connection with the people inside the room.**

How does it feel when you're trying to talk with a friend face-to-face and they're distracted by their screen?

Is it possible that this little device that is supposed to help us connect with others is actually distracting us from connecting with others?

"Just a second, I've gotta answer this text real quick!"

"I've gotta keep my streak going!"

"I'm just posting this for my followers."

We might not intend to be rude, but we're still ignoring the people in the room.

Believe it or not, this is nothing new.

Distractions have always been a problem.

About two thousand years ago two sisters wanted the opportunity to sit and talk with Jesus. One of the sisters did just that. The other sister became too distracted.

The story is in the Bible. It's only five verses long in the book of Luke. It's amazing how relevant the incident is to us today:

> As Jesus and his disciples were on their way, he came to a village where a woman named Martha opened her home to him. She had a sister called Mary, who sat at the Lord's feet listening to what he said. But Martha was distracted by all the preparations that had to be made. She came to him and asked, "Lord, don't you care that my sister has left me to do the work by myself? Tell her to help me!"
>
> "Martha, Martha," the Lord answered, "you are worried and upset about many things, but few things are needed—or indeed only one. Mary has chosen what is better, and it will not be taken away from her." (Luke 10:38–42 NIV)

Mary and Martha wanted to connect with Jesus, so they invited Him over for a meal. Mary sat down and talked with Jesus. Martha was distracted by all the preparations.

Ask yourself: Is there anything wrong with preparing a meal? No. Not at all.

This is where Martha's actions become ironic. Mary and Martha knew that a meal would be the perfect setting to connect with Jesus, but Martha became so distracted by preparing a meal—the very tool she was using to connect with Jesus—that she missed out on connecting with Jesus.

Jesus basically responded, "Martha. . .chill! Order some pizza."

In other words, "Martha, you've allowed your cooking to distract you from the reason you began cooking in the first place. Stop worrying so much about cooking and connect with Me."

Sometimes we might have to say no to good things so we can say yes to better things. Good things can still distract us from what's truly important.

Maybe you first got your phone with good intentions to connect with others, but if you're like most of us, at times you allow it to distract you from connecting with the people closest to you.

REALIZATION #17: Sometimes we allow good things to distract us from what's important.

ASK YOURSELF OR A FRIEND

1. Give an example of how your phone has helped you connect with someone better.

2. Give an example of how your phone has hindered your connection with someone.

3. In the Bible passage, Martha allowed cooking to distract her from connecting with Jesus. What distracts you from connecting with the people you care about?

4. What distracts you from connecting with Jesus?

5. Jesus tells Martha that only "one thing is needed," and Mary chose it. What is this one thing Jesus is talking about?

6. How can you specifically focus on just one thing—your relationship with God—this week?

FINAL THOUGHTS

In that two-thousand-year-old story, a woman named Martha became so distracted by her cooking that it caused her to become "worried and upset." In fact, it even caused her to become bitter and resentful of her sister.

I find this story soooo relevant to us today. Sometimes we enter the world of social media with the desire to connect with others, but once we immerse ourselves in that world, we become overwhelmed by it. It distracts us, it causes us to compare ourselves to others, and before long we just become "worried and upset about many things."

Ask yourself: Is social media becoming a distraction in your life? Is it ironically distracting you from the connections that matter?

What are you going to do about it?

I am not a morning person.

My mom knows this. My siblings know this. All of the roommates I've ever had definitely know this. My dad kind of knows this, although it never stops him from trying to wake me up for a morning run when I'm in town (sorry, Dad, but I don't typically enjoy torturing myself first thing in the morning).

That being said, mornings have historically brought an array of overdramatic events that probably could have been avoided if they happened to me about two hours later into my day.

Needless to say, I have gotten myself into countless conflicts because of my "morning madness." I have never used the term until now, but I'm going with it because it perfectly describes the chaos of life before 9:30 a.m.

Maybe 10:00 a.m.

My poor housemates are the ones who have dealt with it the most. (Shout-out to my current best housemate Anna, who has dealt with my morning madness for almost three years now.)

Unfortunately, some of my housemates found out about my morning madness the hard way.

I have lived in Santa Barbara for the last five years of my life, and it is just as beautiful as it is unaffordable. Yeah. . .it's almost impossible to afford!

So roommates were a given when I moved into my house fresh out of college. That's what you do when you are too poor to have a place of your own. You get roommates and share the bills.

I look back now and laugh because I'm not sure how the three of us shared that tiny room. **We tried our best, but five housemates in one small house and then three girls in one room. . .it was a recipe for drama.**

Like one morning in particular.

I woke up that morning extra happy. Yes, that sentence is an anomaly, but every once in a blue moon you will hear it. I was particularly excited because it was an abnormal weekend when all of my roommates were going to be gone and I had the whole house, and most importantly the whole room, to myself!

It was pure bliss.

With five people in a tiny house, there was rarely a quiet moment. Something was always going on and friends of friends were always over. Being the introvert I am, all of this socializing was rather difficult for me. I had to try to find some time to recharge, but that was almost impossible when sharing a very full house of bubbly twentysomethings.

So, naturally, I took a long, slow morning all to myself. You know—I was on Instagram, sprawled out in bed, unashamed of the double chin I was sporting as I scrolled through my phone. After an hour or two of doing absolutely nothing, I dragged myself out of bed, desperate for coffee. As I shuffled down the hall in my faded T-shirt, fluffy cat shorts, and dingy, used-to-be-pink bunny slippers. . .I noticed something.

I rubbed my face sleepily, probably smudging my overnight zit cream on the back of my hand as I tried to process what I saw. A note was neatly placed on a stack of towels with a homemade cookie in a twine-tied bag. The note was addressed to a name I didn't recognize, instructing this person to make herself at home.

It was signed by one of my roommates.

Make herself at home?

In my home?

In the room that I was supposed to have to myself for the

first time in months?

I snapped. Naturally, I pulled out my phone to text my roommate. I didn't even think; I just started typing.

Why is there a stack of towels with this note on our living room table?

Obviously, I knew why. This was a pointed question, with lots of underlying sass.

I saw the three dots moving and knew she was typing. Then they stopped.

A few minutes later my phone buzzed and I read my roommate's reply: *Ariel is staying over. Didn't you read my message in the group text?*

Ah, the group text. The cursed and oh-so-overused group chat. I had put our house group chat on DO NOT DISTURB mode once when it was furiously vibrating off my desk at work. Sometimes I read all of those texts. Other times I saw a series of animal gifs and decided it probably wasn't urgent enough to demand my attention. Somehow I must have missed the text my roommate had sent.

I looked back through our messages and saw that she had texted us that Ariel would be staying in our room over the weekend while everyone was gone.

But I was not gone.

I was there.

And I was not happy.

Commence morning madness!

I shouldn't have let myself send the next few messages. They weren't blatantly malicious, but they all ended with a period, and let me just say, there were definitely no emojis. At one point I accused her of turning our house into a bed-and-breakfast.

Not my best moment.

Looking back, I realize that my roommate was actually being very kind and hospitable to her friend, providing a place to stay.

I'd do the same. It's the way we should be. But I was too grumpy to see that in the moment.

But even worse, **I had fallen into the trap of trying to resolve conflict through text messages**—which by definition are usually very short and abrupt sentences that are often misunderstood.

After a few minutes of sending these messages back and forth. . .and getting absolutely nowhere. . .we were both angry with each other. You know the conversation has gone too far in text when you start scrolling back to see exactly what was said earlier and then send screenshots of what the other person said.

It definitely wasn't a shining moment for me.

But I'm not going to pretend like I haven't fallen into this trap before. The fact is it is so easy to get sucked into. Nobody picks up the phone to call and just *talk* anymore. That's soooo old-fashioned.

I know I should have called my roommate about this issue (preferably after I allowed myself some time to calm down), but instead I instantly sent a text.

Better yet, I should have sucked it up, endured the weekend, waited until my roommate got home, and talked with her about the whole situation face-to-face. Nothing will create more drama than trying to argue over text.

Here's the crazy thing about texting—and my dad already pointed this out in an earlier chapter. Texting is very misleading. Dad's right: texting doesn't accurately communicate the emotion we're feeling at the time. Sure, we try, with ALL CAPS or a bunch of exclamation marks to try to impress on people *this sentence is serious!!!!* We even add emojis to try to share what our face is feeling at the time.

As fun and convenient as texting is, it sometimes doesn't convey what we're truly feeling. And in heated arguments, it typically only makes things worse.

I learned that the hard way, letting my anger take control

and acting like a five-year-old having a tantrum.

The good news is. . .I learned.

What did I learn? Two simple principles: *wait*, and then *connect face-to-face*. Now when "Grumpy Alyssa" itches to resolve conflict via text or DM, I force myself to delay my response. It's amazing how much wiser I am when I simply wait. And if the person needs an immediate reply, I simply text, *Let's talk later face-to-face.*

Face-to-face is always better.

- -

REALIZATION #18: Texting is a dumb way to try to manage conflict.

- -

ASK YOURSELF OR A FRIEND

1. When are you the grumpiest?

2. Can you think of a time when you got into a "digital disagreement" with someone? How did it work out?

3. Why do you think it's so easy to misunderstand someone through text?

4. What does face-to-face communication bring that digital leaves out?

5. What are the benefits of waiting to respond instead of immediately texting back when angered?

6. Where are some places you can connect with your friends face-to-face and talk through conflict?

FINAL THOUGHTS

Conflict is always difficult. And trying to resolve conflict through texting. . .ridiculous.

Face-to-face wins every time.

I wish it didn't take me so long to learn. But it eventually sank in. In fact, another time when I was working out a tough situation with another friend of mine, after about two texts I just typed, *Hold on, I'm coming over.*

And that's exactly what I did. I drove to her house, gave her a hug, and said, "Let's figure this out." And we did. Afterward I wondered, *Why haven't I always resolved conflict this way?*

What about you?

Two years ago my friends in the town of Paradise, California, lost everything in a fire that wiped out the entire town.

They barely escaped with their lives.

The fire, started by a spark from power lines hitting extremely dry vegetation on a windy day, destroyed nineteen thousand buildings and killed eighty-five people.[1] I live two hours away and the smoke blanketed us for a week.

Fire out of control is terrifying.

Key words: out of control.

I love fire when it's under control. It warms my house. It provides light and a cozy atmosphere. Fire cooks my meals. These are all examples of fire under control.

Fire has to be kept under control!

Californians know fire danger, and if you live in California, you know someone who has had to evacuate their house because of a fire. (Alyssa will share her personal experience with that in the next chapter.)

It's dangerous for one simple reason: it never rains here in the summer—and when I say never, I mean *never*. It rained at the end of May this year and didn't rain again until mid-September. Maybe once in October. Rain usually starts in November.

This consistent summer drought means dry grass and brush everywhere, and just one small spark will start a fire. That's why if you ever watch the evening news in August, September, or

October, you'll hear about some huge California fire destroying thousands of homes. . .like the fire in Paradise.

My friend from Paradise posted a video on Facebook of his family evacuating on the one road out of town through a gauntlet of flames closing in on the small highway. At times smoke enveloped the road so thickly that the hood of the car would disappear, and my friend steered the car with nothing but prayers and hopes the smoke would clear. Five seconds later, seconds that seemed like minutes, the smoke cleared, unveiling buildings on each side of the road engulfed in flames and a lone billboard ablaze.

Truly terrifying. Google "Paradise Camp Fire," and you'll see some of the shocking video.

Fire is greatly beneficial when it's used responsibly in a controlled setting.

Fire destroys when it's out of control.

Perhaps you see the metaphor I'm heading toward. . . .

Our screens can be fun and helpful when they are used responsibly, **but screens can literally ruin lives when used irresponsibly.** The repercussions of irresponsible screen use can be like a fire burning out of control.

I probably witness the negative aftereffects firsthand more than most people because I'm the guy they call after an "incident" that began with a screen. These incidents often start when someone hits POST without thinking twice about the ramifications.

I'm the one who speaks at a school after a young girl commits suicide when her ex-boyfriend sends a revealing pic of her to pretty much the entire school. I'm the one parents consult when their son becomes so addicted to screens that he begins sneaking screen time, until Dad finally happens to see a light under his door at 2:00 a.m. and let's just say both are surprised when Dad opens the door and sees what's on his screen. Or sadly when a young girl ignores all safety precautions, meets a guy on her favorite app, a guy she thought went to the local high school but turns out not to be a high school kid at all, which she doesn't discover until the guy's favorite "uncle" picks her up in his car. . .but there is no kid and there is no uncle—the "kid" was the uncle all along, and the rest of the story is horrific. (True story. Read that again if you must and let that one sink in for a moment.)

Screens can be fun when we use them responsibly.

Screens are dangerous and can damage our relationships with the people we care about when we use them irresponsibly.

Really it comes down to a little thing called self-control. Sometimes our screens will tempt us to look at inappropriate entertainment or engage with destructive influences. These are fires waiting to burn out of control. God's Word warns us to avoid these kinds of influences:

> For the grace of God has appeared that offers salvation to all people. It teaches us to say "No" to ungodliness and worldly passions, and to live self-controlled, upright and godly lives in this present age. (Titus 2:11–12 NIV)

Screens can open up doors to all kinds of "worldly passions." I probably don't need to give you examples, because you already know exactly what I'm talking about. And all of them can lead to hurt.

• •

REALIZATION #19: The irresponsible use of screens can cause repercussions that burn out of control.

• •

ASK YOURSELF OR A FRIEND

1. What are some of the fun or harmless activities you can do with a screen?

2. Do these activities ever become out of control?

3. When do screen activities become dangerous?

4. What are some dangers you've seen that led to hurt?

5. What are some dangers you might need to avoid?

6. How can you be more responsible with your screens?

FINAL THOUGHTS:

Scripture constantly reminds us of that word: self-control. Self-control is even listed as a fruit of the Holy Spirit in Galatians 5. That means when we put our trust in Jesus and give Him control of our life, then others will see the results growing in our life like fruit growing on a healthy tree. "Self-control" is one example of this fruit. Not letting our passions run wild like a fire out of control.

It all starts with putting our trust in Jesus and saying, "Jesus, I need Your help. I give You control."

What are you waiting for?

Alyssa Writes. . .

CHAPTER 20

Terri

I'll never forget December 2017.

It was just a few months after I graduated. I had recently moved into a house with a bunch of other girls, when tragedy struck. . .*twice*. And when I say "tragedy," I'm not talking about running out of data on my phone plan; I'm talking about true natural disasters.

The East Coast has hurricanes, the Midwest has tornadoes. . .California has fires. That's what happens when it doesn't rain every summer for five to seven months. It only takes a spark. But what many people don't realize is that another natural disaster is always quick to follow a California fire.

Mudslides.

In short, fires burn all the vegetation that normally holds all dirt in place with its roots. Come first rain, the enormous volumes of saturated dirt begin to move. . .and literally wipe out entire towns.

In December 2017 my new roommates and I experienced the first natural disaster. The Thomas Fire in Santa Barbara and Ventura Counties burned for almost six weeks before being fully contained mid-January 2018.

It was terrifying.

Little did we know that the worst of it was yet to come.

Many residents evacuated the area during the fires because of the terrible air quality, whether they were in a mandatory evacuation zone or not. The ash was so thick, it fell like snow and covered the surface of Santa Barbara like an ominous gray blanket.

Every day the question was the same: "Do we stay or do we evacuate?" Every day we watched the news and looked at maps. Our little beach house never became an evacuation zone.

Then the rains began, and **unbeknownst to us, the second natural disaster was about to knock on our door.**

I remember the night it happened clearly. I woke up abruptly in my room. My two roommates also stirred in their beds, and I knew I wasn't the only one awakened by the blazing orange color that lit the sky. That and the chorus of our iPhones buzzing from emergency alerts flashing on the screens like a bad dream.

Flooding warning. Stay off roads.

There was a gas leak or something in the midst of the drama of the night. More fires burned, and those were what lit the sky.

I sat up in bed and peered through our dusty, mangled blinds, trying to make out anything abnormal.

Nothing.

Rain beat down aggressively on our roof. I slipped out of bed and nervously paced back and forth in our room. Something was wrong and I knew it, but I didn't know what. It's funny how we are built to sense danger, like a sixth sense really, unexplainable.

My sister was only a few miles away in her college dorm room, and I debated driving up to her. I hated sitting in my house when I felt like something was so wrong. But for some reason, I lay back down and closed my eyes.

Little did I know, choosing *not* to drive up to my sister saved my life.

The next morning we all woke up to messages on our phones alerting us that something had happened.

Mudslide. Homes evacuated. Highway 101 closed. Death toll unknown.

The details were unclear, but luckily I had a cheap HD TV

antenna I had ordered off Amazon that received local channels. We taped up the crude antenna with purple duct tape we had in our kitchen drawer and turned on the news in hopes of seeing what was going on.

The screen confirmed our fears.

Mudslides overnight had surged down Cold Springs Road in Montecito, submerging the surrounding area at incredible speeds, wiping out cars, houses, street signs. . .everything in their path. Hundreds of homes were buried in mud, and many people were unaccounted for. By the time our little town was searched, twenty-one people were found to have been killed during the horrific disaster.

If I had driven up to see my sister the night before, I would have taken Cold Springs Road.

I wouldn't have made it.

I would have been a statistic.

But we couldn't think about that; we had immediate problems to deal with. The freeways were flooded and closed down for miles. **When we looked at the maps the news posted, we quickly realized we were trapped on both sides.** Some of us tried leaving. We got in our cars but within sixty seconds hit roadblocks on all sides. Police apologized to us but pointed to the road behind them buried in three feet of mud. No one could get anywhere without a helicopter.

We were officially quarantined, even worse than I would experience years later during the COVID-19. No one could get in or out. It was just like in the zombie apocalypse movies I had watched with my dad.

Our entire neighborhood rushed to the corner liquor store, the only store we had access to. We bought out all the water and a few snacks. We had no idea how long this situation would last.

Days passed. We kept turning on the news to see if the freeways were open yet and we would be allowed back into the city of Santa Barbara.

Nothing.

Bulldozers were busy clearing away mud miles from our house. They hadn't got to our area yet.

No one was able to work because we couldn't drive to our jobs. No one was able to shower because the tap water was unsafe unless you boiled it. The Wi-Fi was out and so everyone was disconnected unless you had an incredible data plan (which none of us twentysomethings did because we were so poor from trying to live in Santa Barbara). We were left to sit and wait in our houses.

We began going stir-crazy.

After the first day we had deep-cleaned the entire house from corner to corner. I think it was just something to do. It had never been so clean.

It wasn't long before we realized we probably needed to ration the food. So we created a meal plan. My roommates and I took inventory of all our food and came up with meals we would cook together with our combined ingredients we had in the fridge. It was the first time my healthy roommates were grateful that I had terrible eating habits and had nonperishable food stored up in my section of the pantry that would last us for weeks. Macaroni and cheese, tuna, and chicken soup. (Yes, my eating habits were abysmal, but I would survive the next zombie apocalypse with my hoard of imperishable goods. Thanks, Dad! Sorry, Mom, salad is for the weak.)

Day three and we started pacing the halls with nothing to do. Bella and I eventually wandered outside again to stretch our legs. Our neighbors seemed to have the same idea. It seemed like everyone in town was wandering outside, lost and unsure what to do with themselves.

We walked down to the main strip of town where our post office box was. Might as well check the mail, right? There was nothing else to do.

I stepped inside, Bella walking with me, and we noticed people were buzzing all around, chatting about the mudslide and what everyone knew or didn't know about what had happened.

I closed my mailbox in the cramped little room, rubbing elbows with an elderly lady with long silver hair and blue nail polish. She smiled and asked us where we lived. Normally this would seem weird, but everyone here was a local. We were all trapped together.

I told her which house we lived in, and we engaged in polite chitchat as we walked up the hill.

"Terrible thing that happened," she said, shaking her head as she pulled at one of her silver strands of hair with her delicate hand. "I don't know what I'd do if I was driving when that happened."

We had all seen horrifying stories on the news of people who were.

"Makes me glad to be here and not just a few miles that way," she said, gesturing toward the mud-coated roads to our west.

She was right. We were only a couple of miles away. It could have just as easily been us. But our small little town was tucked out of the way, and although we were trapped now, we were safe.

As we got to the next intersection, she stopped and said, "By the way, my name is Terri."

"I'm Alyssa, and this is Bella. So nice to meet you."

"Nice to meet you."

She turned and walked toward her house.

She lived alone, only a few houses away.

As we walked into our house, Bella chuckled to herself.

"What?" I asked.

"It's just that. . .we have a neighbor named Terri. I've lived here for two years, and I just now learned her name."

REALIZATION #20: Sometimes we have a relationship right under our nose that we'll only discover if we put down our screen for a minute.

ASK YOURSELF OR A FRIEND

1. What's the most scared you've ever been?
2. Why do you think most people don't know their neighbors very well today?
3. How well do you know your neighbors?
4. Is there someone in your neighborhood who lives alone?
5. What is something you could do to initiate connection with one of your neighbors?

FINAL THOUGHTS

Those two months were frightening for us, but when we pause and consider what happened to so many people, we realize we were blessed to survive.

It was two weeks before the roads were cleared and I was able to drive up and see my sister who was literally only four miles away. We've never hugged so tight.

Many of our friends lost someone in the mudslide. Horrible stories.

One of our friends was lucky. He pulled up to his house, left his car running, and ran in to get his family. When they emerged from their house. . .the car was gone. Swept away. By God's grace no one was in it.

In those few days, our world was shaken. And during that time, we paused, went on a walk, and met our neighbors.

I met Terri.

As I sit here and write this, I'm thinking, *What's it going to take to get me to go outside again and say hi to one of my neighbors?*

It shouldn't require a mudslide.

I'm going to go take a walk.

"Hello all, I'm taking a break from my phone, emails and all social media for a while."

That was the beginning of Ed Sheeran's shocking post to his 17.3 million Instagram followers when he decided to take a little "digital detox" awhile back.[1]

Ed Sheeran is a talented songwriter and performer with more than 150 million records sold and countless awards. Sheeran is known for his writing, and he found his phone to be a distraction from accomplishing focused work.

I first heard Ed talk about this break from social media on an episode of "Carpool Karaoke" with James Corden. Sheeran shared with James how his phone became really draining and encouraged him to try to do life without a phone.

"I actually don't have a phone anymore," Sheeran said. "I had a phone for like two weeks. . . . I'd wake up every morning and there would be like fifty messages and none of them would say, 'How are you?'; they'd be like, 'Can I have this, can you lend me this, can you do this. . .'"

So Sheeran gave up his phone and internet, using only email (mostly for business).

When he announced to his Instagram followers he would be taking a break from his phone and social media, he described it like this: "I've had such an amazing ride over the last 5 years but I find myself seeing the world through a screen and not my eyes. . . To my family and friends, if you love me you will understand. . . ."[2]

I've met countless people who decided to do the same. *Digital detox.*

It's not that they found digital devices to be evil or wrong. . .just distracting.

The following proverb says it well:

> Look straight ahead, and fix your eyes on what lies before you. Mark out a straight path for your feet; stay on the safe path. Don't get sidetracked; keep your feet from following evil. (Proverbs 4:25–27 NLT)

Are you sidetracked?

I guess that really depends where you're going.

Let's try something.

Pull out a blank piece of paper and follow these instructions very carefully. On the far left side of the sheet of paper near the top write, WHERE I AM. On the far right side of the piece of paper, also near the top, write, WHERE I WANT TO BE.

WHERE I AM ——————— WHERE I WANT TO BE

worrying about my looks —— confident in my identity

No, really. What are you just sitting there for? Pull out a sheet of paper and do it! *Sheesh.*

Now draw a horizontal line from WHERE I AM to WHERE I WANT TO BE. This line represents "the space between."

Now on the far left side of the page under WHERE I AM, write honest descriptions of your life at the moment. Keep these descriptions on the left side of the page in a column. You might write things like *student, soccer player, Christian, play the piano, spend one hour a day watching YouTube.* If you'd like to write some more vulnerable truths, feel free. You don't need to be negative about yourself, just honest. It's okay to write, *I worry about my looks too much,* or *I wish I could quit* _____ *(fill in the blank).*

Now on the far right side of the page under WHERE I WANT TO BE, write honest descriptions of where you'd like to be. Keep these descriptions in a column, trying to leave a gap between your descriptors on the left and your new descriptors on the right. Make each item you write a "glimpse into the future" of what you wrote in the left column. If you wrote *high school student* on the left, on the right you might want to write something like *attending* _____ *college,* or *working as an electrician* on the right. Or if you wrote, *I wish I could quit* _____ on the left, maybe on the right side of the page you write, *now free of*

_____ .

The left column is a description of what your life looks like now.

The right column is a description of what you'd like your life to look like years from now.

Make sense? I'll give you a moment. . . .

Now let's look at "the space between."

The question you're going to ask yourself is "How do I get from here (left column) to there (right column)?" Specifically, "How do I get from being a student now (left column) to attending a certain college or being an electrician (right column) later?"

Write the answer in the middle. You might write, *by studying hard each night and trying to maintain a 3.0 grade point average.* Or "How do I get from worrying too much about my looks (left column) to being confident in my identity (right column)?" Ask yourself, "How do I get from here (left column) to there (right column)?" Maybe you write, *discover who I am*, or *seek who God created me to be.*

This is a good exercise to do with an adult mentor who cares about you. They might be able to help you formulate a plan for achieving your own goals. They also might be able to help you determine some of the *distractions* that could get in the way of these goals you set. Ed Sheeran realized his phone was distracting him from being the writer he wanted to be.

What's distracting you?

- Is social media making you feel worse about yourself when you see what everyone else is posting? Maybe you need to take a break from social media.

- Is Netflix, YouTube, or gaming distracting you from working, studying, or developing meaningful relationships? Maybe you need to limit your screen time.

- Are your screens introducing temptations into your life that are sidetracking you from your relationship with God?

Consider asking a friend to try a digital detox with you. If you find a certain app distracting, maybe it's time for you and your friends to break free from that app. Maybe even use an app that helps you avoid apps. Have you heard of the app "Flora"? Google it. It's an app that helps you and your friends develop self-control and keep away from addictive apps by "planting a digital tree" together, and if any of your friends can't resist. . .the tree is killed!

I know, right?

Do whatever it takes to rid yourself of the distractions that keep you from your goals (see Hebrews 12:1–2).

Is it time to try a digital detox?

ASK YOURSELF OR A FRIEND

1. Who is your favorite musical artist? What is your favorite song? Why?

2. Why do you think Ed got rid of his phone for two years?

3. Have you ever tried taking a break from one of your devices? If so, how was it?

4. Which digital platform (Insta, Netflix, YouTube, etc.) do you find the most distracting?

5. If you ever decided to take a digital detox, what would it look like?

6. When do you want to try it?

FINAL THOUGHTS

As I write this, my cell phone isn't working. Long story, but I switched from one carrier to another and the "switch" didn't happen correctly. So right now the carriers are fighting each other trying to fix it. In the meantime, I'm on my fifth day not being able to receive messages or calls.

It's been awesome!

I've gotten more done in the last five days than in the last few weeks combined.

I'm starting to wonder. . .do I really need a phone?

Do you?

CHAPTER 22

Friend Request from Papa

My grandpa is the wisest man I have ever met in my entire life.

I have always known this to some extent, but at the end of my high school career, I learned this even more so.

My senior year of high school, Papa (I wrote about him in an earlier chapter; that's what I call my grandpa) asked me if he could take me to breakfast before school.

Free breakfast? I wasn't arguing. Plus, I loved my grandpa.

The two of us went to a place about five minutes away from my house called Annie's. It was a little run-down country-style breakfast joint where all the waitresses were at least thirty years my senior. The place could use a deep clean and a little redecorating, but the food was amazing. Everything was slathered in butter, and the pancakes were bigger than my face.

No, really. It was fantastic.

So it became a weekly thing, just Papa and me.

Every week the two of us would go to Annie's, and most weeks I'd put away more food in my five-foot-two-inch frame than Papa would. (Mom, you taught me well.)

Papa was easy to talk to. We'd chat throughout the meal, small stuff mostly. We discussed what I was learning in school, what colleges I was applying to, how my best friend was doing, and so on. Then one day, a couple weeks into it, he got down to the real stuff.

"Alyssa, I don't have a lot of time left with you."

Oh no, I thought to myself. *He's sick, he's going to die, and*

I'm never going to be able to introduce my kids to him! My mind travels to rash conclusions a mile a minute. (I blame you again, Mom, for that habit.)

"You're going to be leaving for college soon, and I'm only going to see you when you're home on breaks."

I let go of the breath I was holding in.

Whew! He was just talking about college. He's okay.

"Alyssa, I want to take you out every week this year on Wednesdays before you leave for college, if you're up for it. And more than that, I'd love to go through a book with you to teach you some principles that might come in handy while you're away at college."

"Of course, Papa, I would love that," I said honestly. "I'm always down to spend more time with you."

He smiled at me and the rest was history. We continued to meet the rest of my senior year and went through a couple of really great books that would prepare me for my next year when I would go away to college. Little did I know that this relationship would be so much more than those breakfasts before school on Wednesday mornings.

Whenever I came home for breaks in college, I would always try to make sure I had time to catch up with Papa. College took quite a toll on my sleeping habits, and I was no longer used to waking up before seven every morning. We swapped out morning breakfasts at Annie's for hazelnut coffees and bear claws at Panera Bread.

These times with my grandpa were so special! Not only did he want to hear all about how I was doing in college, but I was able to confide in him about what was going on, because I knew he always had the best advice. More than that, he was always willing to listen.

And I got to hear all about what was happening at home too. He told me when he and my grandma joined the gym, and

I jumped for joy each time he told me they planned on visiting me at my college. It was always so good to catch up!

I remember one time I was home for holiday break and Papa came over to pick me up for our ritual coffee and catch-up. He pulled out a brand-new iPhone to check on something. He looked like he was struggling with it.

"Papa, you know you can just change this in your iPhone settings, right?" I said, referring to some function he was obviously having a hard time figuring out. I grabbed his phone and changed the setting in just a few taps.

He looked shocked. "Wait, can you show me that again?"

I did it again, but a little slower, explaining what I was doing to get there and fix it.

He smiled, grateful for the help.

"And look, Papa, you can change your screen saver too. You still have the default wallpaper, but come on, you don't want that. That's lame. Watch this."

I took his phone and held it out in front of us as I leaned closer to him to take a selfie of us.

"Smile, Papa!"

I pulled the phone back to look at the photo, and my grandpa peered over my shoulder as I quickly changed the picture we had just taken into his screen saver. **He was beaming as he looked at his new screen saver. Me, with him smiling over my shoulder.**

It was so easy for me, just a few clicks, but it was much more difficult for him.

After that, Papa started asking for my help with little things here and there.

"How do you change this setting, Alyssa?"

"Is there a way to make my alarm go off every Monday at 10:30?"

"Can you help me make this my new profile picture on the Facebook?" (Yes, he calls it "the Facebook.")

It was easy for me, but for him it was a real blessing. I was happy to help, of course—Papa had taught me countless things, sharing his wisdom whenever I would take time to hear it.

And that's the trick. Listening.

Let's be honest—sometimes we aren't the best at sitting down and humbling ourselves enough to admit, "This person probably has some wisdom I could learn from."

Proverbs 2:2–4 (NLT) says it well: "Tune your ears to wisdom, and concentrate on understanding. Cry out for insight, and ask for understanding. Search for them as you would for silver; seek them like hidden treasures."

Hanging out with my papa gave me an opportunity to practice this truth. His knowledge of life continually wows me, and I am so grateful.

And guess what? Every once in a while, I can teach him some of what I know. Especially when it comes to new technology and social habits.

Recently Papa created an Instagram account so he could keep in touch with my sister and me even while we are hundreds of thousands of miles away from him. I showed him how to view "stories" on Instagram, and now he views what all of his grandkids share daily.

Every once in a while, I would get a text from him commenting on something I posted. (I know, I really need to teach him how to DM me directly from My Story.) But I have to say, Papa is my number one hype-man and my greatest Instagram follower. (Watch. A year from now when I get my Instagram back, he will probably have to teach me how to use it!)

What about you?

Are you connecting with your family?

Are you seeking insight and understanding from someone wise beyond your years?

Is there someone in your family who might want to connect with you but maybe thinks you're too busy or is just afraid to ask?

REALIZATION #22: When we seek out face-to-face connections with a wise mentor, everyone benefits from the relationship.

· ·

ASK YOURSELF OR A FRIEND

1. Who is someone in your extended family you feel you can really talk with? Why are they easy to talk with?

2. Is there someone in your family who might want to connect with you? Who?

3. What's keeping you from connecting more?

4. What is a way you can try to connect with them more frequently?

5. What is something you can do today or tomorrow to reach out to this person?

FINAL THOUGHTS

Many young people fled Facebook long ago to avoid being stalked by family.

Kinda sad, if you think about it.

Consider something: in twenty years, you will probably have whole new sets of friends, but you'll still have the same family.

I know, I know, sometimes families can be difficult. My mom came from a highly dysfunctional home. Scary at times. But guess what—she still connects with her dad and her siblings regularly. She and one of her brothers live two thousand miles apart but connect doing a reading plan on their Bible app together. Technology helps them connect.

Connection with family is important.

Is there someone you need to connect with?

Guess what?

My last trip home I saw Papa's phone. His screen saver is still the same pic we took seven years ago, me with him smiling over my shoulder.

Looking hot. You should consider modeling with us. DM me if you're interested.

This is the comment she received on one of her Instagram pics—a pic of her at the lake with her friends. Was the comment really from someone at a modeling agency? She'd actually received quite a few of these comments recently from strangers.

Strangers.

That's a word we don't hear much anymore.

Why?

Because today's social media almost demands followers, and if you have *a bunch* of followers, *a bunch* of them will be strangers.

So how many people your age actually want *a bunch* of followers. . .of whom *a bunch* will be strangers?

The answer is *a bunch.*

In fact, the overwhelming majority of young people want the option to be a social media "influencer" someday. And by majority, I mean 86 percent of young Americans say they want to try out influencing on their social media platforms.[1] Another survey shows 72 percent of Generation Z (if you're under twenty, that's definitely you) want to be online celebs.[2]

But let's say you aren't in that 86 percent or 72 percent who feel a need for more followers. Even if we don't *need* more followers, most of us wouldn't mind having more online friends.

Bottom line: Most of us would like more online friends or followers, and as a result, the overwhelming majority of young people today are a little too casual about who they allow to "follow" them.

Let me give you a real-life example. Several, actually.

Chris. Twelve years old. Playing his favorite game, wearing a headset, talking with a teenager named Jared he met a few months ago and now games with weekly, if not daily. By all definitions, Jared is a stranger. Chris has never met Jared; he has no idea what Jared looks like or how old he is. Jared is just a voice in a headset.

Chris calls Jared a "friend."

Jared makes a comment about a new game system and Chris confesses, "My family can't afford that."

Jared responds, "I'll buy you one. Call it a Christmas present. My dad's rich."

Chris is so excited about the possibility of a new game, he gives Jared his address.

Sure, Chris had heard people say, "Never give out any personal information." But he had played games with Jared for months now. Jared was cool. And his dad was rich.

Fact is, Jared wasn't cool.

His dad wasn't rich.

Jared wasn't even Jared, the police eventually discovered, and he certainly wasn't a teenager. True story.

Then there was Elizabeth. Thirteen years old. Mad at her parents. They told her she couldn't talk with strangers on social media. She thought that was ridiculous. Especially when she met Brian. Brian was a senior at another high school just twenty miles away, and he was the only guy who really seemed to understand Elizabeth. And he shared her love for music.

"He gets me."

The two of them texted every night, sharing playlists.

Elizabeth had never been in love before, but she was pretty sure this was what it felt like. That's why she wasn't suspicious when Brian suggested they finally meet face-to-face for a special "date."

You'll never believe who I have tickets!

Who?!!!

Only the same singer you sent me an entire playlist of last night!

NO WAY!!!!

After dinner out, of course.

Elizabeth told her parents she was hanging out with her friend Alexis, but actually snuck out to meet "Brian." **Sadly, there were no concert tickets, and there was no Brian, just the thirty-seven-year-old creeper who had been communicating with Elizabeth all along.**

I wish I could tell you these were rare occurrences, but they're not. In fact, just a few weeks ago (as I write this) I was at my doctor's office, and the nurse taking my blood pressure asked me what I did for a living. When I told her I was a social researcher who wrote and spoke on internet safety for teenagers, she grew curious and began asking me a bunch of questions. I shared a few of my experiences with teenagers who had met up with strangers they met on social media. When I told her one of my recent experiences, her eyes teared up.

"You know someone, don't you?" I asked.

She nodded and wiped her tears. "My niece. She was trafficked to Las Vegas when she went out to meet some guy who supposedly went to the high school next to her middle school.

Turns out he didn't."

Now whenever I go to speak to a school in any city, I'll jump on Instagram and look at the profiles of some of the kids at the school and immediately check the comments. I find them every time.

Looking hot! DM me if you're interested in making some money.

I have frequently texted screenshots of these comments or links to these profiles to my friend who works at the LAPD in the division to prevent human trafficking.

"Are these what I think they are?" I asked her one time.

"These are rarely who they say they are," she replied. "Modeling agencies aren't scrolling through Instagram profiles desperately looking for 'hot' girls."

Sometimes teenagers will tell me, "Well, apps like Tinder connect people with strangers all the time."

Yes, and did you know that Tinder literally added a "panic" button in early 2020 because so many people got to those meetings and needed help? Adults meeting strange adults need a panic button—or smarter yet, they need to stop using Tinder.

I always warn young people in my school assemblies, "Don't show up at that meeting unless you bring the entire defensive line of your football team with you. Most of the time those people are *not* who they say they are."

Do you know who is following you?

. . . .

REALIZATION #23: If they're nice, they're funny, they're rich, they understand you like no one ever has before, and you still haven't met them face-to-face. . .*they are still a stranger.* Don't go meet strangers, unless you bring ten large friends with you.

. . . .

ASK YOURSELF OR A FRIEND

1. Share about a time you met someone online.

2. Have any of your friends ever met someone online who turned out to be someone different than they said? What happened?

3. Why do you think so many young people don't think it's dangerous to meet a stranger they've been talking to online?

4. Is it ever safe to meet a stranger in person? Explain.

5. What are some ways you can avoid connecting with strangers or, at a bare minimum, better recognize predatory behavior?

FINAL THOUGHTS

As much as we would like to be an Insta-celeb or YouTube influencer someday, these pursuits require followers, and if you allow anyone to be a follower, then you are befriending "strangers."

So what can you do to avoid some creep stalking you or trying to put you in the back of a van?

First, educate yourself about your screens. Little details like "privacy settings" are important, and sadly, most social media apps almost seem to warn you, "If you set this option to PRIVATE, your friends won't be able to find you!" (Which makes you think, *Oh no, none of my friends will find me!* So you leave it set to PUBLIC.) So find out more about how predators stalk young people your age and attempt to "groom" them. *Groom* is a word that basically means to make you feel good emotionally, or to make you feel like you can trust them so you want to be with them more.

Here are some "grooming" behaviors that predators will commonly use:

- Predators are often looking for young people who aren't feeling good about themselves and will make efforts to help you feel better.

- Predators almost always sympathize with the way you are feeling about something and affirm your feelings or choices. *Oh, I hate that. My parents used to say that to me too. You should totally sneak out.*

- Predators often try to drive a wedge in between the young person's relationships with family or friends. *I would never treat you like that.*

- Predators often give excessive compliments or even send gifts or money.

- Predators try to find out your personal information. *I play volleyball too. What school do you play for?*

- Predators may make promises of an exciting, stress-free life custom tailored to your desires. *You know, if you ran away with me, you wouldn't have to worry about money anymore.*

- Predators commonly prey upon young people's sexual curiosity and/or desire for romance, making small sexual comments to see how you respond. *I just took a shower and I'm wearing nothing but a towel.*

- Predators will increasingly introduce sex into the conversation or show you pornography.

- Predators most often will eventually ask for "nudes" or secrets that they will then turn around and use to control you. (I've met countless girls who were blackmailed into finally meeting a stranger because he told her he'd send her nude photo to all her friends and family if she didn't meet.)

If you ever see any of these behaviors from someone online, tell your mom, dad, teacher, or youth pastor immediately. Even if you don't know for sure.

And remember, if you've never met them face-to-face, they're a stranger. Read more true stories about creepy people and how to avoid them in my earlier book, *The Teen's Guide to Social Media and Mobile Devices*.

CHAPTER 24
Weapons of Mass Self-Destruction

You know in the movies when someone is talking bad about their boss or a coworker only to find out that the person walked up behind them? Then they'll always say, "She's standing right behind me, isn't she?"

This doesn't seem to happen in real life very often...but do you know what does?

Accidentally sending a text to the wrong person!

Have you ever sent a text to the wrong person? It's pretty much one of the worst feelings ever.

And no, I'm not talking about when you accidentally spoil your mom's birthday gift, or you text an embarrassing gif to an old classmate in your contacts who has the same name as your sister. Not ideal, but also not the end of the world. I'm talking about those really embarrassing moments when you accidentally text your crush instead of your best friend about how you got to talk to him the other day, and like, he looked soooo good!

Awkward!

Or even worse, you send something nasty about a classmate to your friend, but you accidentally sent it to your classmate!

Don't you wish Tina would shut her big mouth! I mean, seriously, she's such a suck-up to Mrs. Ryan.

Super awkward!

I wish I could say I've never done any of these, but I have. The worst was a few years ago when I had the serendipitous opportunity to work with a really close friend of mine, and she was my supervisor. An interesting element of this work-friend relationship was the need to bounce between friend and boss.

Am I talking with my friend right now, or my boss?

Sometimes it's nice to be able to vent to your friends about a rough day at school or work, but venting to my friend/boss could put her in an awkward position.

One day I was working with a different coworker on a project. He and I had loosely mapped out the tasks for the project and then we were going to divide and conquer. Except that never happened. I ended up carrying most of the load and began to feel very frustrated.

One day I texted him to let him know that I had completed A, B, C, and D, and asked him if we could meet to figure out E together (hoping he could do at least part of E).

The three dots appeared.

He was typing.

Finally, his text appeared. *Oh man, sorry. I can't meet. I've got some other stuff going. But feel free to run any ideas by me.*

In other words: *Sorry, not gonna do E either!*

I was beyond angry.

So I opened a text to my friend/boss.

> Rule number 1: Never text while angry. Not smart. Sadly, I did it.

> Rule number 2: Don't ever gossip about someone else. It's a cowardly move. But I also did this.

> Rule number 3: If you ignore rule number 1 *and* rule number 2, then make sure you text the correct person! I didn't.

I actually screenshot the conversation between me and my frustrating coworker and attempted to paste it into a text to my boss with some harsh words that may or may not have included the word *lazy*. Then I added three upside-down smiley emojis to maturely and eloquently express my frustration with him.

Then I pressed SEND.

I didn't even realize what I had done until I received a reply from my frustrating coworker in ALL CAPS. Let's just say it wasn't very friendly.

I had sent my gossipy rant to him by accident.

I literally dropped my phone, buried my face in my couch cushion (which wasn't wise—that cushion is disgusting), and screamed!

Worst feeling ever.

Have you ever wished someone could invent an UNSEND button?

I know I'm not alone. In fact, a teenage guy who screened this book for us told us, "Last week a girl told me she was mad at me because she was scrolling through her old texts and didn't like something I texted her a year ago. *A year ago!* That stuff doesn't go away."

News flash: your phone doesn't have an UNSEND button. We just need to learn self-control in the first place.

· ·

REALIZATION #24: Phones are like detonators. If you hit the wrong button, everything will blow up.

· ·

ASK YOURSELF OR A FRIEND

1. Have you ever sent something to someone by accident and it wreaked havoc?

2. Has anyone ever sent you something they didn't mean to send you? How did you feel?

3. How "private" do you feel like your phone really is? Are there things on your phone now that you would be worried about someone else seeing?

4. Are there texts or posts you've sent that you wish you could "unsend"?

5. What are some ways you can prevent mistakes like this?

FINAL THOUGHTS

I have always wanted to be a person of integrity.

Integrity. Think about that word. It means authentic, it means honest...it means so much more than that. *Integrity* comes from the same root word as the word *integer.* Do you remember the word *integer* in math? It's a *whole number.*

A person of integrity is whole, undivided, and 100 percent that person. Pure. No dirt. No part of them is something other than what is portrayed.

Consider what that would look like in your life. What if you were 100 percent on the inside what people saw on the outside? What if you were 100 percent on the outside what you were on the inside?

> The integrity of the upright guides them, but the unfaithful are destroyed by their duplicity.
> (Proverbs 11:3 NIV)

Duplicity. That's an accurate description. Dishonest. Fraudulent.

But what if you didn't have to hide a second life because you only lived one authentic life? What if you didn't have to worry about someone hearing you gossip because you didn't gossip? Wouldn't it be nice if someone looked at all your texts, your apps, your browsing history. . .*everything*. . .and you had nothing to hide?

Maybe some of us have some cleaning to do—not of our phones, but of our lives.

In a world where most young people want more followers, it's interesting to see so many celebrities—like the ones with millions of followers—quitting social media.

Hailey Bieber called Instagram a breeding ground for cruelty. Lizzo quit Twitter because of all the haters. Kendall Jenner took weeklong detoxes from Insta.

And they're not alone.

I find it intriguing when people with millions of followers speak out about the pressure social media creates. Like when Hailey Bieber posted a plea to her 24.5 million followers:

> Instagram, Twitter, etc is SUCH a breeding ground for cruelty towards each other, and because people don't take the time to connect with each other on an honest level before they resort to hatred, it starts to damage what could be really beautiful human interaction and connection.[1]

Hailey's comments line up perfectly with what most studies reveal about the effects of social media on our mental health. Many of us have experienced the same thing. Some of us might address it like Hailey did. Others. . .quit.

Like the musician Lizzo, who after having multiple number one songs in 2018 and 2019 just up and quit Twitter.[2]

Why?

Too many haters and trolls.

Trolls, as many of you know, are people who like to

start quarrels on social media. Basically, online gossips.

Lizzo grew tired of the drama that online celeb life was bringing and just quit.

So did comedian Pete Davidson after his breakup with Ariana Grande. He quit Instagram because he couldn't handle the negative comments he was receiving from angry fans.

"No nothing happened," he explained. "No there's nothing cryptic about anything. I just don't wanna be on Instagram anymore. Or on any social media platform. The internet is an evil place and it doesn't make me feel good."[3]

Selena Gomez claims to delete the app from her phone at least once a week because she can't help but read the hurtful remarks.[4]

Prince Harry's wife, Meghan, used to be a big Instagram fan, but after she became engaged to the prince, she deleted her entire social media presence.[5]

> **INTERESTING FACT:**
>
> After two successful seasons of his show, comedian Dave Chappelle walked away in disgust. When asked why, he said, "I like people. I like entertaining. And the higher up I go, for some reason, the less happy I get."*

The examples are too many to name. And we commonly hear the same reasoning: "I couldn't handle the pressure it creates."

Interestingly, Adam Mosseri, the CEO of Instagram, used similar wording when he recently tested hiding "likes." You know, like when your friend posts a picture of her shoes, her cat, or her coffee and gets 287 likes, and then you show a picture of your shoes, your cat, or your coffee and get 53 likes. . .and it's difficult to resist wondering, *Why did Kristen get 287 likes and I only got 53?*

So Instagram tested hiding likes in seven different countries, including parts of the US, claiming the test was to create "a less pressurized environment where people feel comfortable expressing themselves."[6]

The pressure is real.

I feel it.

Alyssa feels it.

Even celebrities feel it.

Do you feel it?

Sometimes social media is like a little barometer of self-esteem. **If we pick up our phone and see a lot of likes on our recent post, then we feel good. If we pick up our phone and don't see a lot of likes, then we feel bad.**

The problem is we keep picking up our phone to take a peek.

It's difficult, I know. It's easy to become wrapped up in how we look to others or in how many people like us. . .when that isn't even where real value lies.

Do you know what God valued when He was looking for a king? It wasn't looks. It wasn't popularity.

> The LORD said to Samuel, "Don't judge by his appearance or height, for I have rejected him. The LORD doesn't see things the way you see them. People judge by outward appearance, but the LORD looks at the heart." (1 Samuel 16:7 NLT)

Are you concerned about your appearance. . .or about who you are inside?

Screens tend to make us focus on outward appearance, popularity, likes, followers. . .it can become an obsession.

That's why Kendall Jenner admitted she took a one-week Insta-detox from her millions of followers. "I just wanted a little break," she confessed. "I would wake up in the morning and look at it first thing. I would go to bed and it would be the last thing I looked at. I felt a little too dependent on it so I wanted to take a minute."[7]

Do you need to take a minute?

ASK YOURSELF OR A FRIEND

1. Who is someone famous you find intriguing? Do you follow them on social media?

2. Why do you think Hailey Bieber described social media as a "breeding ground for cruelty" toward each other? Is she right? Explain.

3. What common reason did most of these celebrities give for quitting social media?

4. Do you think social media creates a pressurized environment for people today? Do you ever feel this pressure?

5. What is some of the advice this book has already given in other chapters to relieve some of this pressure?

6. What does 1 Samuel 16:7 say God looks at? Why do you think He values that more than appearance?

7. What can you do this week to focus more on who you are inside than on your outward appearance?

FINAL THOUGHTS

I have met an increasing number of young people, like Alyssa, who have decided to take a break from social media. Not destroy their phone in a wood chipper, not purge social media for life. . .but simply take a break.

My kids actually instigated this kind of a break in our home when they were teenagers. They had all taken a "media fast" to prepare for a mission trip, and when they got back from the trip, they thought it would be a good idea to take a break just once a week. So our family started "no-tech Tuesdays," which were really more like "no-tech Tuesday evenings."

Their idea!

Every Tuesday, they'd get home and finish homework (using the computer if needed), and then we all went tech-free for the rest of the evening.

We'd read by the fire, eat a big meal, make a fun dessert, go outside with the dog, play a game. . .just no screens.

No-tech Tuesdays.

We loved 'em.

What about you? Do you need a break?

Ever leave a creative voicemail on your friend's phone?

I know, most people don't even leave voicemails anymore. It's much simpler to text. I agree. I text 99 percent of the time when communicating a simple message.

But every once in a while, I like to leave voicemails just for fun!

Let me reiterate something I've mentioned several times in this book so far.

I love my phone!

I have a lot of fun with my phone.

So when you read advice in this book about being careful not to become *enslaved* to your phone, it means just that. Don't become *a slave* to your phone. **You are the phone's master!**

No, phones aren't bad; in fact, they can be quite handy. . . when you're the master. And here's one of those unique ways I've used my phone just for fun!

Rewind ten years ago. I was thirteen and had just gotten my first cell phone.

What is the first thing you do when you get a new phone? Nowadays you might set your new wallpaper or download your favorite apps. Back then it looked a lot different.

My light pink Sony Ericsson slide phone had about five options for wallpaper. And as far as downloading apps goes, there were no apps. This was before smartphones.

What was there to do when setting up your new phone back then?

Setting up the voicemail.

So I had a little fun with it.

Sure, you could be like any boring person and just say, "Hi, this is so and so; please leave your name and number after the beep, yada, yada. . ." Or you could have a little fun and get more creative.

My sister and I were trying homeschooling for the first time in our lives, so we felt a little extra socially deprived. We were left to entertain ourselves in more "creative" ways after we finished all our schoolwork for the day. One of these strange entertainment methods we came up with was inventing creative voicemail messages.

I remember brainstorming with my sister about all the ridiculous voicemail messages we could leave. We would take turns going back and forth trying different ideas. Probably more laughing than talking, actually. If anyone listened in on us while we were recording, they would have heard various ridiculous accents, low- and high-pitched voices, and of course a series of cackles exploding from the room.

We probably did a dozen attempts, trying a new creative option each time.

Finally, as we were recording one, my dad walked in mid-recording.

I had clicked the button and said, "Hi, this is Alyssa McKee," when my dad leaped at the phone and blurted, "GAHHHH!" at the top of his lungs!

I genuinely screamed, hit Stop mid-scream, and then yelled, "Dad!" and punched him in the arm playfully.

He ignored my punch and said, "Well, let's hear it."

I played it back. . .and it was classic!

Greeting. GAHHHH! Genuine scream. Beep.

There was no way we could come up with a better recording than that. And there it stayed as my voice message for the next few years.

Tired of voicemails, we moved on to our next activity, learning to crochet mini scarves for our stuffed animals. (Don't ask me to explain. I was a strange kid.)

But later on in college, I developed a similar habit. (Leaving creative voicemails, not crocheting.) This time, however, it served a better purpose! Whenever my friends didn't answer their phones, I began leaving messages on their voicemail. Sometimes they were pranks where I pretended to be a refrigerator repairman named Cletus. Other times I was in the car on my way to an appointment and I just *had* to tell my roommate a long-drawn-out description of the lady in the car next to me who was scarfing down a Double-Double burger in traffic and dropping it all over her lap (yes, this really happened)!

The habit started as a joke, but as my friends from high school moved away to different places, it started to serve as one of the few ways we could catch up with each other. Texts were fine, but I always felt I could communicate so much more in a voice message.

My friends started returning the favor too. I remember listening to long voice messages from various friends Bluetoothed through my car's speakers while sitting in the parking lot in front of my dorm room, laughing to myself as they elaborated about their day.

My friend Natalie and I particularly thrived through this method of communication. To this day, if she doesn't pick up her phone, I will leave an obnoxiously long voice message for her. I will explain everything I'm doing at the moment until the phone beeps and cuts off my message because I've gone on for too long.

Natalie lives about two thousand miles away from me in Pennsylvania, but she is still one of my closest friends (and you'll probably hear about her again). I owe our continued connection all to my phone.

Thanks, Steve Jobs.

Your devices can help you connect when you learn to use them in the right ways and at the right times. The biggest question you need to ask yourself is this: Is the way I'm using my phone right now helping grow my relationships or harming them?

REALIZATION #26: Phones can provide fun ways to connect with faraway friends.

ASK YOURSELF OR A FRIEND

1. What is the most creative voicemail or answering message you have ever heard?

2. What is one of the most creative or fun ways you laugh and communicate with your friends?

3. How has technology helped you connect with others?

4. What are some ways technology has harmed or could harm your relationships?

5. What is a way you can use technology right now to reach out to someone close to you?

FINAL THOUGHTS

Here are a few of my favorite voicemail messages:

- Hi, this is Alyssa, and since I'm not here, I can take a message. Hold on, I'm looking for a pen (*sounds of rummaging through a drawer*). Just a second, it's gotta be here somewhere (*more rummaging*). Hey—that's where that went. I've been looking for that forever. . . . Oh, hold on, still no pen (*more sounds*). Aha! Found one. Okay. Go ahead! *Beeeep.*

- Hi, this is Alyssa McKee, and I'm...uh (*flushing sound*)...busy at the moment. Leave your info. *Beeeep.*

- Speak! *Beeeep.*

- (*In my best movie preview voice*) In a world where Alyssa is occupied, one person can leave a message. *Beeeep.*

- (*In my best Yoda voice*) Leave a message you will. Do, or do not. There is no try. *Beeeep.*

- Hello? Hold on...I've got a bad connection. Okay, that's better, I can hear you now. What's up? (*Long silence*) Did you really fall for that? *Beeeep.*

- Think fast! *Beeeep.*

- You've reached movie phone. If you know the name of the movie you'd like to see, press 1. If you know the name of the local theater, press 2. If you live in a shoe box, press 3.

- Hi, this is Alyssa McKee—GAHHHH! Aaaaaagh!!! *Beeeep.*

The world mourned when Kobe Bryant died, and Shaquille O'Neal immediately began connecting with friends and reconciling.

The death of a friend affects us all in different ways. For Shaq, it reminded him of the urgency of making things right.

January 26, 2020, was a tragic day for sports fans when a helicopter crashed in Southern California, killing nine people, including basketball legend Kobe Bryant and his daughter Gianna. Kobe and his daughter were traveling to her basketball game when the helicopter crashed, killing all on board.

Shaq was working out with his sons when he heard the news. He didn't want to believe it.

"Please don't be true. Please don't be true. Please don't be true," Shaq told himself, hoping it was a hoax.

It's no secret that Shaq and Kobe used to have a very competitive relationship, even throwing a few punches at each other once in a pickup game.[1] But they had recently made up, and Shaq is grateful.

But Kobe's death triggered something in Shaq. It triggered the desire to connect with friends he'd had disagreements with. So he picked up the phone and started reaching out to them.

"Hey, man, I love you!"

Shaq recorded his podcast the next day, sharing some of his feelings about his relationship with Kobe.

"I wish I would've communicated more," Shaq admitted.[2]

It was too late with Kobe. But it wasn't too late with everyone else. Shaq called his best friend the same day and made promises to check in on his friends more consistently. Shaq said Bryant's death was a wake-up call to not take those you love and respect for granted.[3]

Shaq was compelled to reconcile some of his relationships. He didn't want to leave conflict unresolved. This is a principle Jesus taught in His famous Sermon on the Mount:

> "So if you are presenting a sacrifice at the altar in the Temple and you suddenly remember that someone has something against you, leave your sacrifice there at the altar. Go and be reconciled to that person. Then come and offer your sacrifice to God." (Matthew 5:23–24 NLT)

Jesus wants us to resolve conflict—and to do so immediately. Bryant's death reminded Shaq of the importance of making things right. In fact, Shaq felt guilt for not reaching out to his friends more than he did.

"I just really now have to take time and call and say I love you," Shaq said. "I'm gonna try to do a better job of just reaching out and just talking to other people rather than always procrastinating because you never know."[4]

You never know.

* *

REALIZATION #27: Life is too short
to leave conflict unresolved.

* *

ASK YOURSELF OR A FRIEND

1. Have you ever lost a friend or loved one?

2. Is there anything you wish you would have said or done before they passed?

3. Why do you think Shaq picked up the phone and started calling people the day Kobe died?

4. Why is reconciliation so important?

5. Why do you think Jesus tells us to reconcile with others before worshipping Him?

6. Is there someone you need to reconcile with? What are you waiting for?

FINAL THOUGHTS

My close friend just lost his mother—she died suddenly, without warning.

The last conversation he had with her was a fight and he hung up on her.

When she died, the first thing he said was "We never made up," and he started crying.

Don't leave conflict unresolved.

Get face-to-face with people if you can. If not, pick up the phone. But don't just leave it alone.

CHAPTER 28

Apps for Days

So many apps, so little time!

Over the years I've slowly realized that having too many apps stresses me out. More apps means endless notifications and annoying reminders telling me I need to pay attention to them. Maybe I don't want to pay attention to you, app that distracts me daily, telling me someone I haven't seen in three years posted a picture of their salad. I just don't need to be notified of that!

Let's be honest—notifications are a pain.

At first, the obsessive-compulsive region of my brain would demand I look at all these notifications each and every day so the irritating red dots would disappear.

I can't stand those red dots!

Surely some app developer must know this, luring me to open the app and investigate each one of them. (Yes, if you paid attention earlier in the book, my dad mentioned that app creators do this on purpose so your brain will release dopamine and you'll crave more notifications, spending even more time on their app.) And that's exactly what happens each time I click on a notification. I become distracted for way too long looking at my aunt's new puppy, my friend Christine's new shoes, my friend Brian's Disneyland photos, Jasmine's candid selfie—Jasmine with her perfect skin—Jordan's enormous burger at In-N-Out. . .mmm—yum!

Three minutes of scrolling and I'm jealous of shoes, perfect skin. . .and even puppies. And also hungry for some In-N-Out!

These distractions became a daily frustration.

Notifications.

Click.

Scroll.

Feeling jealous.

Feeling hangry.

Sometimes this daily ritual would turn into twenty or thirty minutes!

One day I'd had enough. I was tired of being a slave to my notifications, so I simply began three practices:

1. *First, I turned off all notifications.* This was so refreshing. I suggest trying it. This simple step relieved so much anxiety and saved me an average of fifteen minutes a day. . .fifteen wasted minutes that I'd never get back. But it didn't clean up my clutter of apps. So I did something else. . . .

2. *I organized my apps into natural categories.* My categories include games, social media, music, TV, and travel (part of my job is getting on flights, renting cars, staying in hotels, etc.). Some people like categories, and some don't. For me, they helped me feel more organized and cleaned up the clutter. But then I took it a step further. . . .

3. *Every few months I open each of my categories, reorganize, and delete apps I don't use.* This new habit of reorganization helps me consider what I need to focus on and what I need to forget. I ask myself, Do I really use this app? I mean, honestly, I haven't ever opened it once since I initially downloaded it. Delete! I'm amazed how refreshing it feels to actually delete something.

Delete the Tap Tap Fish game. I played that game for three straight hours once and then never used it again.

Delete the Hulu app. My free trial expired, and let's be real—I don't have the time or the money for another subscription, and I already spend enough time on Netflix.

Slide the Nike running app to the front page of my phone. Maybe that will motivate me. . . .

These three simple practices have actually reduced stress and anxiety in my life.

Read that again.

Taking a few minutes each month to organize my phone has saved me hours each month. . .*and it has reduced anxiety*.

I don't know if you've been watching the news, but depression, anxiety, and even suicide attempts among young people are all at an unprecedented high right now as I write this. They all spiked right around the time that we all began carrying smartphones and social media in our pockets.

A pocket full of stress.

But it doesn't have to be that way.

Our phones don't have to enslave us.

You don't have to check every notification.

You don't have to get sucked into the black hole of "click and scroll."

· ·

REALIZATION #28: Some apps on our phone can help us, but other ones can hurt us. Taking time to organize our apps is worth the effort.

· ·

ASK YOURSELF OR A FRIEND

1. When was the last time you cleaned out your phone apps?

2. What are some apps you have that are very helpful and improve your life?

3. What are some apps that might be more harmful than helpful?

4. What is one app you want to download that might help you improve your life?

5. What is one app you probably should delete? Why? So when are you going to delete it?

FINAL THOUGHTS

I'm about to do something in this book that I haven't done yet: I'm going to write two chapters in a row!

Why?

Because I want to make a point.

Your devices can help you or hurt you. It's up to you to decide which. In this chapter we talked about trimming away some of the distracting or even harmful apps. But not all apps are harmful. In the next chapter we'll talk about some apps that actually *help* you connect.

CHAPTER 29
From Opposite Sides of the Planet

My little sister, Ashley (twenty-two years old), came back to California to visit me recently, but the experience was bittersweet.

The bitter part is because Ashley's husband, Joe, was just deployed to Afghanistan with his unit in the army. This is going to be a tough nine months for Ash. She really misses Joe.

Ash met Joe in our middle school group at church when she was just eleven, and the two of them have basically liked each other on and off for a decade. They went to school dances together, and then Ash would like Joe, but Joe wouldn't like Ash. Then Joe *would* like Ash, but Ash wouldn't like Joe. Finally, in college Joe told Ash, "You're the one." And after only two more breakups, they got married. Their story is admittedly romantic.

And now, thanks to a screen, Ash and Joe get to talk to each other from opposite sides of the planet.

This week while Ash was visiting, we were hanging out together drinking our favorite coffee when her phone rang that unique ringtone. Her face lit up.

"It's Joe! He's FaceTiming me."

A click of a button and there was Joe, sitting in his army fatigues giving Ash his normal greeting. "Hey, baby girl!"

Video chat is pretty amazing when you think about it.

If one of your grandparents served overseas in the military, communication was only through letters.

Can you imagine?

Yes, screens can actually help relationships when you can't get face-to-face.

APPS THAT CONNECT

My guess is that you've discovered aspects of technology that have helped you connect with family and friends. I have countless guy friends who connect with their buddies regularly from whatever location to battle each other to the death (thank goodness I'm talking about a video game).

For these guys it's a bonding thing. It's not really about gameplay or cool graphics (although those definitely make it fun); for these guys it's a chance to hang out together via modern technology doing something fun.

The high school girls I meet with each week do the same with their social media. Sometimes they'll send a story just to me or a small group of friends, showing us something funny that happened to them or even sharing something impactful from their day. I only see these girls in person once a week, so screens are actually the majority of our connection. **These screen connections don't replace our face-to-face connections; they fill in the gaps in between.**

In each of these situations people use screens as a means of meaningful connection.

And that's just it. Sometimes screens can actually help you connect.

We said something earlier in the book and I'll say it again. Screens can be a great way to connect with people outside the room, but only when they don't cause you to ignore the people inside the room.

What are the apps that help you connect, but not disconnect?

I've really been enjoying an app called Marco Polo. My friend Natalie, whom I mentioned in an earlier chapter, uses Marco Polo to reach me from over two thousand miles away in Pennsylvania. We used to leave each other voice messages all the time, but Marco Polo has made it a little more fun because we can leave each other long video messages, and it allows me to see her face.

Sure, I could FaceTime her or something live, but with the time zone difference (she's three hours ahead of me) and crazy conflicting schedules, sometimes it's nice to be able to leave a message and go back and forth at our own pace.

I ended up loving this app so much that I told my other long-distance friends about it too (no, these aren't people I met online, but actual face-to-face friends who moved away). The app has now allowed me to connect with friends I love who live miles away. Now I can feel a little more a part of their lives!

Screens can be helpful when you can't connect face-to-face. Maybe you experienced this during the COVID-19 pandemic. Screens were one of the only ways to connect with those outside the home. But even then, most young people became frustrated that they couldn't connect in person. "Screens only" got old pretty fast. Even though teenagers were spending far more time connecting digitally with each other, 48 percent of them said they felt "less connected with friends" during those weeks, according to a survey from Common Sense Media.[1] Sometimes extended separation from friends and family makes us realize how good "face-to-face" really is.

But when you can't get face-to-face, screens can help connect the disconnect.

REALIZATION #29: Screens can actually help our relationships when we can't get face-to-face.

ASK YOURSELF OR A FRIEND

1. What is an app, game, or online tool that has helped you connect with others? Give an example.

2. Could this app also become a distraction and disconnect you from others? How can people avoid disconnect?

3. Have you ever been separated from your friends for an extended time and were only able to use digital communication? How does digital communication compare with face-to-face?

4. What is something you can do this week to connect with someone you can't speak with face-to-face?

5. How can you avoid disconnecting yourself from those close by while you're using a screen to connect with others far away?

FINAL THOUGHTS

Have you ever heard of the app Spaceteam?

Neither had I.

This app looks like *Galaga*, *Space Invaders*, or some other ancient video game my dad played as a kid (and that was a long time ago, folks!). It's very pixelated with the most ridiculous throwback sound effects.

But here's the great thing about the game: you *have* to play with other people. And the more people you play with, the more entertaining!

You link up phones through Wi-Fi and you are transported into space in your very own ship. However, you don't control your own ship—you have to shout out commands to your friends and work together as a space team! (Just try it. You'll see.)

There is much yelling and laughing when playing this game. I remember once in college playing the game with one of my roommates. Our third roommate, Maddie, came in as we were yelling commands at each other in British accents, trying not to laugh so we could hear each other's commands. Maddie immediately demanded to play. She quickly downloaded the app, and we played together on our lofted dorm room beds for the next hour or so, our homework lying on the floor and collecting dust.

The best part is later that day we kept talking in our fake British accents, commanding each other to *pass the salt directly adjacent to the pepper*. And to *duck—meteoroids ahead!*

We were united in conversation by this silly game we had played on our phones for debatably way too long. But for once our phones led us to come together instead of pulling us apart into our own little worlds.

How cool is that?

Screens pulled us together.

A fun little app called Spaceteam actually pulled us together.

Yes, screens can actually help you connect.

Jonathan Writes. . .

CHAPTER 30
McKee Annual Christmas Pageant

We tried it randomly a few years ago, and now it's a family tradition.

We call it the McKee Christmas Pageant, and it's a pretty big deal in our house. We even have a trophy. It happens the day after Christmas, and everyone participates.

The first year the assignment was simple: everyone comes up with a Christmas performance, no longer than five minutes, and the word *sweatpants* must be included in the script (don't ask. . .there's really no logical reason behind it).

Our family really gets into it, even the shy members. Probably because the audience is strictly family: kids, parents, grandparents, aunts, uncles, cousins. Everyone does a performance.

Alyssa and Ashley did a dance routine.

It was awesome!

They mixed several songs together, and at one point in their routine, they stopped and shouted, "Sweatpants!" Then the dance resumed.

My wife and I did a skit about a babysitter and the baby. She was the babysitter and—you guessed it—I was the baby. (I actually wore a diaper.) We had a special guest cameo in that skit that year—my daughter's fiancé at the time, Joe. It was a test. He married her anyway despite how weird her family is.

The next year we each had to do a scene from a movie, but with a creative twist. It was hard to top the year prior, but the performances were hilarious. (I still remember Alyssa's portrayal of Gollum. Oscar winning!)

This past year we added the trophy. *One trophy that rules them all.* The rules were to tell the original Christmas story in a creative way. The best performance wins the trophy and keeps it until the following year. My wife, Lori, and I did a modern musical. I'll spare you the details, but we each burst out in song, with occasional tweaks to the lyrics. The audience was pretty generous, because we took home the trophy!

Here's the thing: it's the day after Christmas, the family is together, being creative, laughing, and cheering each other on. It's pretty cool. **Waaaay better than just sitting around staring at screens.**

And let me tell you, this is a screen-loving bunch! My brother and I have both worked on film sets. I majored in film and now do movie and entertainment reviews. My nephew makes movies with his iPad. My daughter Ashley is a history major and binges Netflix documentaries like no one I've known.

We love our screens!

But the day after Christmas, you don't see anyone sitting in front of a screen. Everyone is interacting and practicing their performances until finally. . .evening brings the start of the McKee Annual Christmas Pageant.

I'm not implying you need to do a Christmas pageant. I'm just glad our family found an activity that provokes so much face-to-face interaction and encouragement. Holidays can be full of these moments. . .even if your family structure looks very different.

Take my good friend "Dan" for example. He's divorced and has two daughters who float between two houses: Mom during the week, Dad on the weekend. He desperately wants to spend time with his daughters, so every time they're together, he plans activities that provide plenty of face-to-face interaction.

If you're a young person reading this, you might be thinking,

But I'm just a kid! Kids don't plan the events. Adults do. I can't tell our family we're going to "interact face-to-face"! Maybe you're even thinking, *My parents are always looking at their screens and they wouldn't want to do any face-to-face activities!*

Don't underestimate the power of your voice. The Bible backs you up on this: "Don't let anyone think less of you because you are young. Be an example to all believers in what you say, in the way you live, in your love, your faith, and your purity" (1 Timothy 4:12 NLT).

Most of you have way more influence than you think. I don't know a lot of parents who wouldn't respond to their kids' request to put down screens and do something fun. It doesn't have to be the "Smith Annual Christmas Pageant" (assuming your last name is Smith. . .that would be kind of weird if your last name was Wiley). Think of some of the ordinary everyday ways you could connect with your family:

- Think of an outdoor activity you enjoy and organize a time to go do it: hunting, fishing, biking, hiking, playing disc golf. . .the options are limitless.

- Think of a place you and your parents, grandparents, brothers, and sisters all like to eat and suggest connecting there for dinner—no screens allowed. If some dinner places are too expensive, try finding something affordable, a fast-food place where you can just order fries and drinks.

- Find some board games or card games that your family might like playing together—games that get everyone sitting around and talking with each other (our family loves Phase 10, Euchre, Scattergories, and Bananagrams).

- Find a book you and your family might enjoy together and ask if you can read it together as a family before bed: the Lord of the Rings trilogy, The Chronicles of Narnia series, *The Zombie Apocalypse Survival Guide for Teenagers.* . . .

Just find something that motivates your family members to put down their screens and engage in face-to-face interaction. And if you want. . .give away a trophy!

REALIZATION #30: Holidays can be a great time to instigate activities that prompt the entire family to put screens away and interact face-to-face.

ASK YOURSELF OR A FRIEND

1. What does your typical Thanksgiving, Christmas, or Easter look like with your family? How much face-to-face interaction is there?

2. Being honest, are you someone who encourages interaction or who retreats to screens?

3. How open would your family be to trying more face-to-face family activities?

4. What is a face-to-face activity that your mom, dad, or other family member has been wanting to do that you have resisted in the past? Would it be so bad to try it?

5. What is one face-to-face family activity you can suggest this week?

FINAL THOUGHTS

Alyssa's friend "Danielle" was raised by a single mom who worked two jobs. But no matter how busy she was—and single moms are busy, y'all—she always made time for her daughter.

When Alyssa visited Danielle one Christmas, she and her mom were decorating Christmas cookies.

"Perfect timing," Danielle said when Alyssa arrived. "We're

just about to do the frosting."

Alyssa walked in to see trays of fresh-baked cookies blanketing every countertop. Danielle's mom was putting another batch in the oven.

"Join us!" she said with a smile.

Within five minutes they were all spreading red frosting over little Santa-shaped cookies and decorating the tiny faces with various candies and sprinkles. They laughed hysterically while licking gobs of frosting from a spoon, all to the tune of Nat King Cole.

"This is fun," Alyssa declared, stating the obvious. "Do you do this every year?"

"Every year," Danielle said, biting off Santa's head with a smile.

No trophies. No embarrassing skits. But a fun Christmas tradition that Danielle and her mom looked forward to every year. . .*with no screens in sight*.

CHAPTER 31
Caught Red-Handed

Have you ever done something really stupid at school right when your teacher was walking by? Or if you've had a job—same thing—right when your boss was walking by?

When I was seventeen, I was bored at work, so instead of entering the data I was supposed to be entering at my desktop, I began texting my friends. True story—feet on the desk, staring at my phone, I blew a bubble with my gum, and my boss walked up and just stared at me.

My bubble popped! (Perfect timing.)

I quickly set my phone down and went back to work like nothing happened. My boss walked away shaking her head. . .leaving me to simmer in my shame.

I thought that was as bad as it could get.

But a few years later I did one better. . .er. . .worse. Imagine the same scenario as above, but this time your boss could also see exactly what you were texting.

Worse, right? Yeah, that happened to me.

Except I am a grown-ish woman, so minus the bubble gum and feet on the desk. Replace the phone with my giant computer screen and the text messages with Google Hangout messages on my Gmail screen.

Adult location, same stupid teenage mistake. Will I ever grow up? (Seven years later and I'm still messing up. If I could use an emoji right now, I would insert the girl face-planting her hand abashedly.)

It started like a normal workday. I came in and made myself a coffee and a Pop-Tart (I have a powder-blue toaster in my cubicle, nbd). Then I turned on my computer, went straight to my emails, and started working away. A couple of hours into working, I was drafting a new email when I saw a flash of green in the corner of my screen. It was a new chat message from my coworker Linnie, so I tapped on it to expand her message.

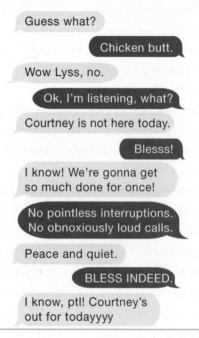

Guess what?

Chicken butt.

Wow Lyss, no.

Ok, I'm listening, what?

Courtney is not here today.

Blesss!

I know! We're gonna get so much done for once!

No pointless interruptions. No obnoxiously loud calls.

Peace and quiet.

BLESS INDEED.

I know, ptl! Courtney's out for todayyyy

I was deep in the conversation, bopping back and forth to my music slightly, when I heard something and swiveled in my chair to look over my shoulder.

My boss Mario was standing behind me.

"Hey, Alyssa, have you emailed Tiffany Thompson yet? We need to follow up with her."

Mario said this as I swiftly collapsed my messages and looked at him intently, pretending I was fully focused and interested. Meanwhile, my heart was pounding. That was close!

I started responding to Mario when I heard a soft ping, and out of the corner of my eye I saw a green glow flash again.

Crap.

My body took mindless control over my head, and against my better judgment, I turned to peek at the messages springing up on my screen. Not very smart, I now realize, thinking about it. I might as well have pointed my finger directly at the screen.

Linnie had messaged me again, **and all of our gossip flashed brightly on the monitor like a beacon** beckoning Mario closer toward the screen. And that's exactly what happened. I caught my boss leaning closer, his eyes scanning the screen, reading the messages with a furrowed brow.

My stomach dropped, and I heard myself let out a soft awkward laugh. (Again, thinking back on it, not the time for laughter.)

Mario obviously had read enough. He let out a quick, "Hmm," and simply turned around and walked out of my cubicle. No remark about how disappointed he was. Not a word. Just a disappointed sigh, and he was done with me.

The guilt was overwhelming.

I immediately headed outside, grabbing my coworker who had engaged in the gossip with me, dragging her out as well. I told her what had happened. Our boss Mario had seen our messages and was obviously not impressed.

"Noooo," Linnie said, closing her eyes in agony.

We leaned against the stone bridge outside our office across the way, our heads hanging down as we stared at the ground, shifting our feet back and forth on the dirt path. We were silent for a while.

"Now what?" Linnie said, looking at me with a concerned face.

But that was just it: there was nothing to *do* because we couldn't *undo* it. Our cruel words were out there, and they couldn't be taken back. No matter how we could have tried to justify our feelings, we had used our words to tear someone down, and it was a terrible feeling.

Here's the funny thing: my first reaction was *Oh man, I got caught! I really need to be more careful what I'm typing at work.*

But honestly, "typing" wasn't the problem.

Gossiping was the problem.

If I wasn't talking about others in the first place, then I wouldn't have to be careful what I typed.

· ·

REALIZATION #31: If you don't want to get in trouble for throwing shade. . .then don't throw shade!

· ·

ASK YOURSELF OR A FRIEND

1. Is there a time when you ever got caught gossiping about someone else? How did you feel when you got caught? Was it worth it?

2. How can screens add to the detriment of gossip in our lives?

3. What's easier, typing gossip or saying it out loud?

4. What is one arena in your life where it's most tempting to gossip?

5. What are some creative ways to prevent this temptation?

FINAL THOUGHTS

Frankly, I'm glad I got caught.

I deserved to feel as guilty as I did for talking the way I did about one of my coworkers.

The sad thing: that coworker is a friend. Is she irritating at times? Yes, but aren't we all? And she's still a friend. It's just never okay to talk negatively about others.

Sometimes we talk about people and think they *deserve* it. That doesn't matter. We need to control what leaves our mouth. The Bible shares this truth throughout, but James makes it crystal clear: "If you claim to be religious but don't control your tongue, you are fooling yourself, and your religion is worthless" (James 1:26 NLT).

At the end of the day, our words should only ever be used to pump people up, not tear them down. And if our words are not working toward good for someone or some purpose, then they shouldn't be said at all.

CHAPTER 32
Attack of the Killer Squirrels

A few years ago, I encountered a creepy little squirrel when we bought our property up in the foothills of the Sierra Mountains.

This critter was mean!

Come to think of it, he probably was just angry because I refused to feed him.

The previous owner liked squirrels, feeding them every morning from the front porch. Imagine the little furballs' surprise when the old owner was gone and so was their food source.

I realized this one day when a particularly aggressive little squirrel started chattering at me. At first I thought it was just a loud bird, but then he scurried toward me, cursing me from behind his four nasty little teeth. (Fun fact: squirrels have just four teeth that grow constantly so they can constantly gnaw on things.)

I tried to ignore him, but he followed me.

True story.

He darted toward me, chattering like he was cursing me out. (It was kind of freaky!) When I tried to walk away, he followed, lunging toward me. I stomped my feet at him, but he only took a few steps back, then scurried forward again. It was something out of a horror film! I actually took off running, and the squirrel chased after me. I finally escaped to my garage (hoping no one saw me running from a squirrel).

Squirrels are a lot more aggressive than many people realize. They are extremely territorial and will fight other squirrels to the death when defending their area. A quick search on YouTube will deliver limitless clips of squirrels attacking each other. . .and even attacking people!

Yes, savage suicidal squirrels!

Squirrels aren't wimps. They can run up to 20 miles per hour and have padding on their feet that provides cushion when they land jumps of over 20 feet.[1] (I'm a little jealous.)

Bottom line: Don't make enemies with a squirrel. They might kamikaze you from a tree when you exit your house! (Not really, but it would make a great horror movie.)

I didn't want to deal with squirrels bullying me for nuts, so I decided to do something about it. I went down to the local animal shelter and brought home two cats: Smokey Robinson and MJ (Smokey is gray, and MJ is black and white—don't read into it too much). The two of them became fast friends with my dog Lionel Richie.

It wasn't long before the two cats began hunting. And these two are awesome hunters. Each morning we'll find gifts of mice, lizards, birds, partially eaten snakes. . .even bats. Smokey and MJ are warriors.

Their favorite meal is definitely lizards. I'm no zoologist, but I have my theory why. Lizards are easy to catch! I've seen countless lizards lying on my patio, doing their little push-up maneuver or lethargically basking in the sun. Every time my cats catch sight of one of these clueless reptiles, it's dinnertime. Smokey or MJ will just creep up behind the resting lizard and pounce.

Game over.

Interestingly enough, my cats have never caught a squirrel.

As talented hunters as my cats are, the squirrels' large eyes on each side of their head always see danger coming. They can spot predators approaching from far off, and they scurry to safety every time.

Squirrels see approaching predators.

Lizards, the ones on my patio anyway, become waaaay too comfortable and don't even see approaching danger.

Squirrels—completely aware.

Lizards—clueless.

That begs the question: Are you a squirrel or a lizard?

Are you aware of the dangers out there? Or are you becoming waaaay too comfortable with your surroundings, so much so that you don't even see approaching danger?

I ask this because most of you have access to a device that is smart, efficient, fun. . .but also exposes you to a world of immense danger. And sadly, many people today don't even see it coming. I know, because whenever I counsel young people who are experiencing the consequences of a decision they made with their phone or on social media, **the first words out of their mouth are always, "I didn't know. . ."**

"I didn't know he wasn't who he said he was."

"I didn't know she would tell other people."

"I didn't know he knew where I was at all times whenever I used that app."

"I didn't know she would post that."

"I didn't know he would show that picture to other people."

"I didn't know. . ."

None of them saw danger coming.

Do you?

Let me be clear. This book is full of examples of ways our screens can become a distraction from wise living. And yes, even though our devices can be used for many good things, let's be honest—at times our screens can become dangerous:

- Screens provide access to raunchy entertainment, even porn.

- Screens offer easy connections to bad influences.

- Screens expose us to cyberbullying.

- Screens connect us to some people who want to physically harm us.

- Screens tempt us to laugh at others, post mean posts, and make rude comments.

- Screens sometimes just distract us from the things we should be doing.

Are screens always dangerous?

Yes, in about two clicks.

Screens are like a car. You can be driving safely down the road but then with one simple swerve of the wheel start heading the wrong direction, a place where dangers lurk like a lion ready to pounce.

A lion is a good analogy. Maybe that's why the Bible uses it: "Stay alert! Watch out for your great enemy, the devil. He prowls around like a roaring lion, looking for someone to devour. Stand firm against him, and be strong in your faith" (1 Peter 5:8–9 NLT).

My two cats prowl around my backyard looking for prey.

Squirrels are very aware of the danger.

Lizards never see them coming.

Are you a squirrel or a lizard?

REALIZATION #32: Many of us become so comfortable with our screens that we don't even recognize danger.

ASK YOURSELF OR A FRIEND

1. If you could have any pet, what would you have? Why?

2. Why do you think Peter compared the devil to a lion?

3. What does Peter tell us to do? What does he mean by "stand firm"?

4. What are some of the dangers lurking on our screens?

5. How can you "stand firm" against some of these dangers?

6. What is one way you can practice "standing firm" this week?

FINAL THOUGHTS

Are you conscious of where you're wandering on your screens, or are you completely ignorant of the cat lurking behind a nearby tree?

Next time you're on your favorite device, I'd like you to think like a squirrel.

No, squirrels are not the most glamorous animals, but they're very aware!

Are you aware?

In the next chapter we'll talk about one very specific area where we can apply this vigilance. . .and by specific area, I mean an area you are very familiar with, because you go there each and every night.

Earlier in the book Alyssa wrote two chapters in a row, and now it's my turn, because I can't think of a more important topic to talk about than how screens affect sleep, and sleep affects *everything*!

I'm not exaggerating.

The sleep you get tonight affects almost everything about your tomorrow. Not just your alertness for tests, or your attitude around the people you love, but especially your mental health.

Yep, you read that right. Going to bed later can actually make you feel sad and hopeless.

The research is crystal clear. And I think you might be surprised exactly how important every hour of sleep is: "In a study of nearly 28,000 high school students, scientists found that each hour of lost sleep was associated with a 38 percent increase in the risk of feeling sad or hopeless, and a 58 percent increase in suicide attempts."[1] Think about that for a moment. When you go to bed, if you pull out your phone and stay up an extra hour playing games or scrolling through your favorite social media, that loss of sleep has a huge cost, especially in the area of mental health.

That's why **if you went to see a doctor or counselor about depression, one of the first questions they'd ask you would be about your sleep.**

Why?

The American Academy of Pediatrics concludes, "Addressing

insomnia will greatly improve treatment of depression."[2]

Sleep is vital.

And if sleep is a problem, guess what the doctor's next question will be?

"Do you keep any screens in your bedroom at night?"[3]

So it's like this:

Screens in Bedroom = Less Sleep = High Risk of Depression

I know, I know. Chances are, you don't want to hear this. And trust me, I don't really want to be the one who has to tell you, because you might not like me giving you the bad news. (Have you heard the expression "Don't shoot the messenger"?)

But you and I have spent an entire book together, and this subject is soooo important, I'm risking "likability" points by telling you the truth. And so instead of trying to tell you what to do, I'm going to do you the favor of simply giving you the information. What you do with this information is up to you.

Here's the most current research about screens and sleep:

- 79 percent of teenagers bring their screen into the bedroom each night, 70 percent use it within thirty minutes of going to sleep, and 36 percent wake up at least once to check a notification or social media, getting even less sleep.[4]

- The percentage of teens who are constantly sleep deprived jumped to 43 percent (a 22 percent jump) once the majority of teens in America got smartphones (and those numbers rise with each hour spent online daily). Screens are the biggest cause of sleep deprivation.[5]

- The American Academy of Pediatrics (AAP) has been recommending "no screens in the bedroom" since before 2010,[6] before you even had your own screen, and their advice hasn't changed. In fact, now they also recommend avoiding exposure to screens one hour before bedtime.[7]

- The National Sleep Foundation reveals that lack of sleep makes you more prone to pimples, illness, and aggressive behavior, and limits your ability to learn or recall information (which makes taking tests a lot more difficult).[8]

- A study out of the University of Texas Health Science Center revealed teens are four times as likely to be depressed if they are sleep deprived[9] (and, as I shared at the beginning of this chapter, have a 58 percent increase in suicide attempts[10]).

The studies are honestly too vast to list, so let me summarize. As a guy who studies this stuff all the time, allow me to let you in on a little secret: researchers are still debating things like "How many hours should kids be on their screens each day?" and "How much social media is too much?" But the one thing that almost every researcher agrees on is *no screens in the bedroom*.

Jim Steyer, CEO of Common Sense Media, summarizes it well: "There are times and places where phones should not be there. The bedroom is the obvious one."[11]

It's your choice:

> *Option A:* Leave your phone in the bedroom and expose yourself to less sleep and a greater risk of depression, suicide, acne, illness, aggressive behavior, lower grades. . .the list goes on.

> *Option B:* Charge your phone in another room. . .and you can check your phone in the morning!

> Hmm. . .

REALIZATION #33: Phones are like caffeine—
they seriously mess with your sleep!

ASK YOURSELF OR A FRIEND

1. Why do you think 79 percent of young people keep their phone in the bedroom all night even though doctors have been recommending against it for more than a decade?

2. Does the fact that 79 percent of your friends have their phones in their rooms all night make it more difficult for you not to have it all night?

3. What are some convincing reasons Jonathan provided to show that phones don't belong in the bedroom?

4. Are there any reasons you feel the need to keep your phone in your room overnight? Is doing so wise?

5. What is a step you can take with screens this week to ensure better sleep?

FINAL THOUGHTS

Here's the thing. Young people who end up on their screens hours upon hours into the night end up regretting it.

Read that sentence again.

Years later they truly look back and say, "I wish I would have. . ."

So ask yourself truthfully:

- Does my phone, tablet, computer, or game system keep me up, even a little bit, most nights?

- Do I check my messages after I go to bed? In the middle of the night?

- Do I ever end up wandering into places I shouldn't go on my screens at night?

Did you answer yes to any of the above questions? These are all symptoms of being enslaved to your phone, and freedom is only about twenty feet away (assuming your room isn't bigger than twenty feet).

Try this.

Tonight, turn off your phone or set it to DO NOT DISTURB mode (no sound, no vibration), and plug it in somewhere outside your room where you won't be tempted to look at it in the middle of the night. If you find yourself getting up to look at it, then consider asking your mom or dad to charge it for you in their bedroom.

Then before bed, take out a pad of paper, a blank book, or a journal, and write down your thoughts about the day. Write a prayer if you want. Do something to replace the "media" activity you used to do at that time.

Maybe even pull out your Bible and open it to a passage like Psalm 119. Each night read just a few verses and think about what that looks like in your life.

> Joyful are people of integrity, who follow the in-
> structions of the LORD. Joyful are those who obey
> his laws and search for him with all their hearts. They
> do not compromise with evil, and they walk only in
> his paths. (Psalm 119:1–3 NLT)

Ask, *What is this scripture passage saying to me?* I need to do what that first verse says: follow the Lord's instructions. *How?* Doing what the second verse says: searching for Him with all my heart. *What does that look like?* Doing what the third verse says: not compromising with evil.

Hmm. *Follow God's instructions, seek Him with my heart, and don't give in to evil temptations.* That's pretty wise counsel for using our screens.

That's pretty wise counsel for bedtime.

That's pretty wise counsel for life.

Have you ever been rejected?

This year a bunch of my close friends and I were all rejected by a group of guys. Actually, *rejected* is too kind a word. We were snubbed. Completely ignored. It was as if we weren't even there.

The sad part? These were friends! And they chose *Fortnite* over us.

It started when we all gathered at my friend Christine's house for a fun evening with just us girls! We were all in our twenties, most of us graduated from college, a few in college still, and we decided to cook dinner together.

About an hour into the night as we were laughing and cutting vegetables, we heard a knock on the door. A group of guys we knew surprised us, saying, "Hey, can we hang with you?"

We didn't mind. It actually sounded kind of fun. Don't get me wrong—I like hanging with my girls, but we didn't really have any expectations for the night, so we welcomed them in.

It wasn't five minutes before they discovered a game console. "Oh cool! Check it out!"

Within minutes all the guys were **gathered around a screen playing a game, while all the girls worked in the kitchen.**

This turn of events wasn't cool.

I try not to always bring up "girl power" or shift conversations toward women's rights, unequal pay, all that unfair stuff that happens all the time. . .but come on, this was just too obvious! Girls in the kitchen while the guys sat on their backsides? Uh, no.

One of us walked over and said, "Hey guys, wanna help?"

I'm not making this up—not even one of them acknowledged us. They were so immersed in the game, it was like they all thought maybe someone else would answer.

No one did.

This was a really nice group of girls, so no one got too unraveled. But then we needed to get out a platter for a veggie tray, and the platter was in a cabinet one of the guys was leaning against over by the TV. My friend walked over and said, "Excuse me really quick—I need to grab something."

Again, nothing.

She stood there for a few moments while the rest of us girls watched, standing there silently as the boys continued to play. Literally another one of my friends stopped chopping carrots and we all just stared.

"Excuse me!" she said, a little louder this time.

The guy didn't say a word, just moved a couple of inches, never taking his eyes off the screen!

Okay, guys, let me give you some quick advice. I understand video games take a lot of focus, especially if you want to do really well. I've played countless games with my brother. And I understand that maybe these guys just wanted to relax, and this was their way of relaxing. But here's the deal: these guys were our guests. . .and they were snubbing us! This is basic manners 101. You don't ignore people when they talk to you. Especially when you are a guest in *their* house!

And for you guys reading this, I truly wish I could include a picture of the girls in this room. I'm not one to toot my own horn, but for my friends I totally will. *These were pretty girls!* Now, of course prettiness doesn't indicate value or affect the way someone should be treated—I'll be the first to tell you that. I'm telling you this simply so you realize these guys weren't just rude—they were blind!

Since when is it okay to snub anyone?

Since when is it okay to snub someone when you are their guest?

Since when is it okay to snub someone after you just came over uninvited?

Here's the funny thing. None of us overreacted. None of us went over and switched off the TV (although honestly, I should have). We actually just let it play out. Maybe we were thinking when they joined us for dinner, we'd mention something. And that's where the situation got really hilarious. Soon one of them looked at their watch, and then they all got up, mumbled goodbye, and left.

They just left.

It didn't really matter to us because we were happy to have "girls' night" back again. But one of my friends ended up saying, "Those were the stupidest guys I've ever met!"

We all burst out laughing.

None of us could argue with that.

· ·

REALIZATION #34: Too often, video
games seem to lobotomize guys.

· ·

ASK YOURSELF OR A FRIEND

1. Have you ever been snubbed by someone focused on a screen? How did it make you feel?

2. Have you ever snubbed someone by refusing to take your focus off a screen? How did that work out?

3. What do you think these guys were thinking?

4. What should they have been thinking?

5. Is there a screen activity that might distract you so much that you don't even realize you're disrespecting someone?

FINAL THOUGHTS

I don't know if those guys ever realized what they did.

None of us ever said anything.

But I do secretly hope one of them reads this book and realizes, *That was me. I'm Stupid Guy No. 3.*

Well, Stupid Guy No. 3, I forgive you. But sorry, none of those girls are ever going to date you.

CHAPTER 35

Five Songs That Make You Think

A few months ago, Common Sense Media surveyed eight- to eighteen-year-olds and asked them what activity they enjoyed most with their screens.[1] You might be surprised at the results.

Even though social media, gaming, and watching videos on YouTube were high on their lists. . .*listening to music* ranked highest among teenagers, even more so among girls.

And now that our music collection is conveniently accessible in our back pocket, we are listening to more and more of it each year. Think about it. It's almost always within reach. I know every time I get into the car with a bunch of teenagers, one of the first things they ask is "Can I plug in?" Next thing we know we're listening to one of their playlists through the car speakers.

And playlists are fun.

One of the things I loved the most about driving my car in high school (actually, it was my parents' car and I got to drive it every once in a while) was that I had control of the radio!

Back then cars only had radios and tape decks (this was before iPhones, iPods, even before CDs. . .yes, I'm *that* old). So I always brought a few tapes with me in the car so I could listen to the music I wanted to hear.

I remember one particular album from a Christian musician I had heard in concert. His name was Steve Taylor and his music was very innovative for the time. One of his songs was titled "Drive, He Said," and it was the story of a man driving a car who picked up a hitchhiker. But it didn't turn out to be just any hitchhiker;

it was someone creepy who knew every little detail about this man. As the song played out, you realized this hitchhiker might not have been a man at all, but an evil entity.

Here's the thing: **Every time I played this song, my friends would always stop talking and listen.** Then they would ask questions.

"Wait, did he just say he owned the man?"

"Did he just pick up the devil?"

Finally, we'd be asking each other, "What would you do if the devil was trying to get you to sell your soul?"

That song always had a way of grabbing us and catalyzing conversation.

And that's just it. Sometimes music proves to be much more than just background noise. Music can resonate with us. Music evokes emotion. Music can even connect you to others.

Music is powerful.

Yeah, I know. Sometimes we listen to songs just to relax or escape. I'm with you. That's a fun aspect of music. Most of the time when my friends and I listened to music, we just turned it up and zoned out. But sometimes music does much more. . . .

Do you ever craft a playlist that sets a certain mood?

I've got a playlist titled "Vegetate."

I've got another one titled "Angst."

I titled one "Lori" because it makes me think of my wife.

I've got one titled "Riding in the car with Thom" because it's all the music my brother used to play in the car when we were kids. I played it for him this Christmas, and immediately we began reflecting on times when we were driving together, places we went.

Music can trigger nostalgia.

Does music ever stir your emotions?

Here are five random songs that always make me pause and think. Who knows—they might even provoke fascinating face-to-face conversations.

"EVERYTHING I WANTED" BY BILLIE EILISH

In 2019 Billie Eilish released a compelling song titled "Everything I Wanted," and her fans loved it!

Eilish's unique image and sound drew quick attention—she isn't your typical pop star. But her music is what really captured the world's focus. She swept the Grammys in early 2020 like no one her age has ever accomplished.

Even if you don't necessarily enjoy Billie Eilish's music, you'll probably admit the lyrics to this song are intriguing. "Everything I Wanted" is based on one of her real-life dreams, one that impacted her so deeply she and her brother Finneas wrote a song about it. The song tells the story of how she dreamed she committed suicide and no one cared or even noticed. But then the song takes an intriguing turn. She wakes up and realizes there is someone who actually cares for her (in real life, this was her brother).

This caring person says, "As long as I'm here, no one can hurt you," and goes on to say, "If I could change the way you see yourself," encouraging her to see all the good in herself that he sees.

This song seems to resonate with people for several reasons: First, a lot of people wonder if there are others who truly care for them. Second, most of us would love someone to be there for us and say, "As long as I'm here, no one can hurt you," not to mention seeing the good in us, noticing our potential, and liking us for who we are.

Aren't those things that you long for too?

ASK YOURSELF OR A FRIEND

1. Have you ever felt unnoticed and unloved? When?

2. Do you have someone in your life who cares for you and wouldn't let anyone hurt you?

3. Who sees the good in you, notices your potential, and likes you for who you are?

4. How does God feel about you? (Reread the passage Alyssa shared in chapter 8, "Liar, Liar," from Psalm 139.)

"EVEN IF" BY MERCYME

MercyMe is a Christian band whose songs have been inspiring people for literally two decades ever since the release of their very first crossover single, "I Can Only Imagine" (and if you haven't seen the powerful movie by the same title, I encourage you to check it out).

"Even If" is one of my favorite songs from the band, an honest conversation with God during a tough time, a time when they admit, "A little faith is all I have right now."

The power of the song is in the background story, an inspiring moment from the book of Daniel, chapter 3, when three young boys, Shadrach, Meshach, and Abednego, are about to be burned alive in a fiery furnace by the evil king Nebuchadnezzar, who wanted them to worship his false gods. When the king threatened to throw them in the fire, they replied:

> "O Nebuchadnezzar, we do not need to defend ourselves before you. If we are thrown into the blazing furnace, the God whom we serve is able to save us. He will rescue us from your power, Your Majesty. But *even if* he doesn't, we want to make it clear to you, Your Majesty, that we will never serve your gods or worship the gold statue you have set up." (Daniel 3:16–18 NLT, emphasis mine)

In this song, Bart Millard, the lead singer, confesses some modern-day struggles where he is weak, but then he declares that he knows God is able to save him—but even if He doesn't, he *still* hopes in God alone.

ASK YOURSELF OR A FRIEND

1. When is a time you've felt, "A little faith is all I have right now"?

2. What is MercyMe saying when they sing, "Even if You don't" save me from these tough times right now, "my hope is You alone"?

3. Name a time when it is difficult to be faithful to God during tough circumstances.

4. Why do you think MercyMe finishes the song by singing, "It is well with my soul, it is well with my soul, it is well, it is well with my soul"? (Google the story behind the old hymn "It Is Well with My Soul.")

"GOD ONLY KNOWS" BY FOR KING & COUNTRY

"God Only Knows" is not only a powerful song but also a powerful music video, and in a world where most of us have access to screens, I'm going to suggest you quickly search for the music video and watch it.

Many of us will identify with the words of the song, including phrases like "nobody sees you," and with living a life where we feel like no one understands what it's like to be us.

The music video follows a girl who wakes up obviously feeling alone and carrying the weight of something. She gets up regardless, puts on her makeup, and even practices a quick fake smile, one we see her use throughout the day.

Who can relate?

Here's where the message of the chorus is clear: God alone knows everything you've been through; He knows what other people say behind your back; and He alone knows that it's tearing you apart on the inside.

Eventually the girl in the video has had enough and she

escapes her friends and finds her way onto the edge of a bridge to take her own life. That's where the video takes a turn. I won't spoil it for you; you'll have to watch it yourself. It's powerful.

The chorus of the song shares the idea that there is a unique and special kind of love that only comes from God. It's followed by the idea of a new beginning. . .a brand-new start. . .

And the video reveals what that might look like. A restart.

ASK YOURSELF OR A FRIEND

1. Have you ever felt like no one knows what you're going through?

2. Have you ever considered that there are others who are thinking, *No one knows what I'm going through*?

3. How did the friend in the video reach out to her friend?

4. How can we reach out to someone who is hurting?

5. What do you hear God saying to you through this song?

"YELLOW" BY COLDPLAY

Have you ever put on sunglasses with a yellow tint?

Have you ever put on sunglasses with a gray tint?

It's amazing to see how a simple tint completely changes how you see the world. A yellow tint makes everything look bright, sunny, and cheery. . .and gray does exactly the opposite. Completely dreary.

Coldplay's breakthrough hit, "Yellow," starts with the simple claim, "Look at the stars, look how they shine for you, and everything you do. . ."

I always liked the song, but I think it really connected with me when my daughter Ashley heard me listening to it and said, "I love that song!"

"Why?" I asked her.

"It just makes me feel loved!" she said.
Stars, shining for you. . .and they were all yellow.
Makes me feel loved.

ASK YOURSELF OR A FRIEND

1. What do you think of when you look up at the stars and just stare at them for a while?

2. Why do you think Jonathan's daughter Ashley said the song made her feel loved?

3. What makes you feel loved?

4. Read Psalm 8:3–4. What do you think David was feeling when he looked at the night sky?

5. How much does God truly love you? (See Romans 5:8.)

"EVERYTHING GLORIOUS" BY DAVID CROWDER BAND

This song is a simple prayer, a true praise song that helps us realize our value.

The message is simple: "Hey, God, if everything You make is glorious, and You made me. . .I guess I'm glorious!"

ASK YOURSELF OR A FRIEND

1. Sunsets, waterfalls, horses running through a meadow, the ocean crashing on the sand. . . What is something in God's creation that you think is truly glorious?

2. How can a relationship with Jesus make the day and night "brighter"?

3. How can you reflect God's glory in your life today?

FINAL THOUGHTS

It's funny if you think of it, but today many people judge someone's value based on a few numbers.

- How many followers do you have?
- How many "friends" do you have?
- How many likes did you receive on that post?

The math is simple: A lot of likes means you are valuable. Not many likes. . .well. . . A lot of followers means you have influence. Not many followers. . .well. . .

One of the elements I like about the songs in this chapter is the conversations they each provoke about "value." In a world where most of us struggle with feelings of insecurity, God reveals a totally different perspective on value.

"I wouldn't let anyone hurt you."

"I'm here for you during tough times."

"I know what you're going through and I love you."

"I value you more than all the stars in the heavens."

"I made you glorious!"

Alyssa Writes...

CHAPTER 36
Todd Chamberlin

Everyone has someone in their life who they can't help but smile around. Someone who is confident in the way they walk, talk, think, and laugh. Someone who causes you to grin in a way that no one else does. This is the kind of person you happen across only a few times throughout your entire life.

For me, one of these people was a guy I'll call "Todd Chamberlin," a friend I had back in high school.

Everybody liked Todd, but not for the reasons you'd think. He wasn't a jock with chiseled abs or a model with perfect hair and skin. He actually was pretty normal looking. In fact, he didn't really care what he looked like. His clothes looked like hand-me-downs from his older brother, hanging off his body awkwardly, and he confidently wore sandals typically found on the feet of sixty-five-year-old men. All this he wore proudly, his hair freshly styled by his pillowcase that morning.

He exuded this joyful, happy-go-lucky confidence in every aspect of his life, not just the way he appeared. His taste in food and entertainment was nonconforming. His humor was random, perhaps even a little bizarre. And he had a gift for making everyone else laugh.

Funny, Todd went against anything and everything that was currently popular, but not in the typical rebellious type of nonconformity. Todd just seemed to enjoy that which was unique. Often we would be driving in my car, my sister in the back leaning toward the front the way she always did when Todd was riding shotgun. He would always turn off whatever pop songs were typically spilling from the radio and would instead plug in and play songs at least twenty years old—stuff my dad liked! Sometimes he'd be belting "Rocket Man," singing along with Elton John at full volume, missing half the lyrics. . .but Todd didn't care. His voice was terrible, but his smile was huge. He was so happy we were all smiling with him. His joy was infectious, and we wanted to be part of whatever random thing he was up to next, regardless how strange it was.

And that's what was so interesting. Todd wasn't worried about what people thought of him, but people were truly drawn toward Todd.

Todd wasn't trending on social media, because Todd didn't post anything on social media.

Todd didn't worry about how many online "followers" he had, and interestingly enough, he had plenty of real-life followers because he was just plain fun.

It's not that Todd didn't like screens. He actually really enjoyed movies and music. But when you watched a movie with Todd, you ended up discussing it with him in great detail afterward. Whenever you were in a room with Todd, he was fully engaged with you.

And Todd was just random. For my birthday one year, Todd came over with a handful of items. He thrust them into my arms with a wide grin on his face and a quick "Happy Birthday!" One of the items was a crudely molded rat he had made from clay and fired in ceramics class. Another item was a mild sauce packet from Taco Bell that said, "I'm my favorite too." A third item was a Wonder Woman pullover sweatshirt that said SUPER. He also gave me a short story he had written, folded up on notebook paper that he had obviously torn out of his math notebook because algebra problems were scribbled on the back in blue ink (they were solved wrong, but that's not the point). And last but not least, there was a wallet-size picture of himself, smiling with a dog I didn't recognize on his lap. The dog, he explained later, belonged to his friend from across the street, and he had taken his senior portraits with the dog because he just thought it was the funniest-looking dog ever.

Strange as the collection of gifts was, it was genuine. I loved it and I look back at it fondly as the best assortment of birthday gifts I ever received.

There were a lot of great things about Todd, but the greatest thing was just that he wasn't caught up in trying to be *something*. He was genuinely himself no matter what, and although it was raw, often sloppy, and sometimes ridiculous, he fully embraced it with a smile on his face. . .and his smile was contagious.

I don't see Todd much anymore—we live in different cities— but I'll never forget the fun times I had with him.

Todd was always genuinely Todd. . .and people liked him for it.

· ·

REALIZATION #36: People would probably like me more if I was just me.

· ·

ASK YOURSELF OR A FRIEND

1. Have you ever encountered people who were truly happy just being themselves? Describe them.

2. What is something fun or interesting about yourself— maybe a talent, hobby, or taste in something—that most people don't know?

3. Why don't you let people know about this aspect of yourself?

4. What makes you smile?

5. Think of someone close to you: a friend or family member. What makes them smile?

6. How can you connect with someone and make them feel "fully engaged" this week?

FINAL THOUGHTS

One of the interesting things about Todd Chamberlin was his ability to make you feel noticed and heard. When you were with Todd, you never felt like an observer. He wasn't buried in his phone like everyone else. He always made you feel present and a participant.

Todd engaged people face-to-face.

What does that actually look like?

My papa is really good at "engaging" people, making them feel noticed and heard. In the next chapter, my dad will share how Papa actually does that.

Would you like to know the secret to becoming liked?

Actually, I'm misleading you by calling it a "secret," because it's not some mystery potion you ingest or a sketchy app you can purchase to boost your likability; it's just a proven habit you can practice that will enhance your face-to-face relationships. And it's a word you probably weren't even allowed to say when you were growing up.

Just *shut up*. (Okay, it's two words.)

It's true. Most of us don't realize the power in just shutting our mouths and listening to someone else. It not only makes people like you better; it makes them feel closer to you.

I learned it from my dad (Alyssa's papa). My dad is a master listener.

Once my dad went to a Christmas party at the college where my mom was an English professor. He didn't know anyone in the entire room, so he began walking up and introducing himself. Every time he would say, "Hi, I'm Tom. I don't think I've met you yet."

And they would always introduce themselves. "Hi, I'm Linda. Good to meet you."

And that's when my dad would begin sculpting his master-piece: *the fine art of shutting up*. This delicate dance is always accomplished by asking questions. Questions keep the other person talking.

"Do you work here in the English department?" he would ask.

"No, my husband does," she'd reply. "I'm just along for the ride. Ha-ha."

"So what do you do?" my dad would ask.

"I'm a social worker who works with foster kids in Placer County."

"Wow," my dad would say. "That's such a needed vocation. How did you get into that?"

And the conversation would go on for five to ten minutes. He'd always say just a few words in the form of a question, and the other person would begin baring their soul!

My dad would do this the entire night.

He'd talk with a dozen people, just asking questions and listening, never talking about himself. And here's the funny thing: When my mom would go to work the next day, all these random people would walk up to her and say, "I met your husband. He's the nicest guy." And then they'd all ask my mom the exact same question. "What is it that he does, anyway? Is he a professor?"

Do you know why they'd ask her that?

They never asked him *a single question* the night of the party. My dad just kept them talking about themselves. When the party was over, all they could think was *That guy was nice. I wonder what he does.* They *wanted* to know more about him.

My dad understands something about people: **people love to be noticed and heard.**

In fact, some people have *no one* in their life who listens to them. Not a single person! Most people don't listen. Like the wise proverb says, "Fools have no interest in understanding; they only want to air their own opinions" (Proverbs 18:2 NLT).

Imagine if you actually were quiet enough to attempt to understand someone else. People love when someone notices them and listens to their heart.

Last week (as I sit here and write this) I saw this truth play out on the middle school campus by my house. I dropped by to see the principal and hang out with kids during lunch. The first kid I saw was engrossed in his phone.

"Let me guess," I said. "*Fortnite*?"

"No." He laughed. "But I do like *Fortnite*."

A kid standing near him said, "I play *Fortnite* all the time."

"Me too," another kid chimed in, and started doing a *Fortnite* dance move.

This started a chain reaction.

"*Watch me!*"

"*Yeah, but can you do this?*"

"*I can. Watch!*"

"*I can too.*"

And that's about all I heard for the next five minutes. . .

"*I. . .*"

"*I. . .*"

"*I. . .*"

Why? Because everyone wants to be noticed and heard. So, sadly, everyone tries to direct the conversation toward themselves.

Here's the funny thing. I was on campus for three lunches and I didn't hear one kid express interest in one of their friends and ask, "Oh really? That's cool. When did you learn to do that?" Everybody was too busy saying, "Watch this!" or "Guess what I did!" "I. . .I. . .I. . ."

Everybody wants to be noticed and heard.

But the simple truth is that showing interest in others is the best way to get others to take notice of you.

· ·

REALIZATION #37: If we shut up, stop talking about ourselves, look people in the eye, and just ask them questions. . .we'll make a lot of friends.

· ·

ASK YOURSELF OR A FRIEND

1. Who is someone you know who is a good listener? How do they make you feel?

2. Why do people like being noticed and heard?

3. What does Proverbs 18:2 say fools have no interest in? What does that mean?

4. How can you attempt to "understand" others?

5. Who is someone you know who doesn't get noticed or heard very much?

6. How can you "engage" them?

FINAL THOUGHTS

When I was in high school, I wasn't very popular or athletic...but I was a really good listener. I would look up from whatever I was doing, look people in the eye, and listen.

I remember when Whitney Brown sat next to me in government class. She didn't have a clue who I was. And I never told her. I just *listened to her.*

She would come into class and say, "I can't wait for this class to be over!"

"I know, right?" I'd say. "What class do you have next?"

"Psychology."

"Do you like it?"

"It's okay. It helps me understand my idiotic boyfriend."

"Ha. Like what?"

I would keep this up every government class for the entire year. And pretty soon, she was talking with me more than she would talk to any of her friends. In fact, she told me something that I heard from many girls during high school: "I can really talk with you!"

That's because my dad had taught me *the fine art of shutting up.*

I'll always remember my first kiss.

If only it was as good as his texts.

I don't know quite when I realized I was boy-crazy, but it probably goes back to first grade when I set my eyes on my first crush. We'll call him "Alex Whitman." He was a twin, and Annie, my best friend and neighbor two houses down, liked his brother. So, naturally, I *had* to like Alex. And let's face it—I was infatuated with the idea of getting married and living with my best friend and our husbands. (Annie told me twins live together forever, so obviously all four of us would share a conjoined house.)

Annie and I planned all of our lives together from our double wedding down to the names of each of our children. Of course, we never talked to the twins; that was completely unnecessary. We simply dreamed about our lives together from afar, drawing pictures of our houses and gazing at the boys across the class-room tables as we squished play dough in our hands.

Next came "Matthew Wilson." I switched elementary schools in fourth grade and was nervous I wouldn't make any friends. But when I set my eyes on the freckled, redheaded boy with green eyes sitting in the front row of our classroom, I quickly decided that switching schools was fate and Matthew and I were meant to be together.

I chased him on the playground at school and whispered to my friends about him in line on the way to lunch, our purple and pink lunch boxes swinging back and forth as we snickered about our crushes. This crush continued through sixth grade, and I even stayed up late at night with my sister, staring at our class pictures and drawing hearts around his freckled face squished in the middle of the other chubby sixth graders.

But my love was ruined near the end of my sixth-grade year when during recess Matthew gave "Brooke Sheldrake" a heart-shaped necklace (one of those fancy plastic pink ones from Claire's). The necklace was an obvious sign of his adoration, and I was devastated to see him give his heart away to another woman. Dang that Brooke and her beautiful blond hair and Abercrombie jeans. I would never be able to compete with that!

Junior high was a series of similar crushes, admiring the boys from a distance and never receiving reciprocated adoration. It wasn't until my freshman year of high school that boys started to notice me (maybe it had to do with the graduation from my sports bras and my redemption from braces, but who really knows for sure).

I know I wrote in an earlier chapter about my first boyfriend, "Danny Romano," but Danny was my first *boyfriend*, not my first *kiss*. My first kiss was with a boy I met at school; we'll call him "Trent Harrison." I had noticed him from afar, and he must have noticed me too, because he flirtatiously started texting me out of the blue. He was athletic with spiky dark hair, and he was *very* interested in me.

What else did a girl want? Am I right?

I would soon find out. . . .

Trent had expressed his interest in me in the suavest way possible. . .*over text message.*

I could tell by the way he confidently texted me, he was effortlessly cool!

His words were brief. His punctuation casual, but not too irresponsible. The perfect ratio of emojis. This guy was the coolest guy I had ever talked with.

Well. . .I hadn't actually talked with him.

Only texted.

But I didn't care. His texts said it all!

I was once again glued to my pink slide phone, anticipating message after message and eventually deciding I needed to seal the deal with this boy. I had never been kissed yet, but in my high school brain, I knew that was the way you became boyfriend and girlfriend. And his messages to me were so forward and so smooth, he obviously knew what he was doing.

So, naturally, we decided we needed to plan our kiss.

Via text.

True story. We actually texted about it in anticipation, trying to find a time when we would be able to meet (very smooth and subtle, I know). Then the opportunity arose. One of my friends, who happened to go to his church, invited me to one of their youth group activities that Friday night.

Perfect.

I remember the night clearly. I wore my neon-blue V-neck top and my sister's soccer sweats, an outfit that I thought looked super cool but now realize was oddly casual in anticipation of a first kiss.

Then I saw him.

He saw me.

We both walked different directions. Talking in person was a little weird. So we didn't. At all.

The entire night!

The night went on and we avoided each other perfectly, hanging out with everyone but each other and avoiding prolonged eye contact. Had to play it cool, obviously.

We went through the entire night without interacting, until it was almost time for everyone to leave. I was hanging with some friends and wondering if I would ever get the opportunity to kiss Trent. As I walked to the bathroom, I saw Trent and his friends from a distance, chasing each other all over the church playing with giant Nerf Blasters that could surely kill a small animal. As I walked down a hallway by myself, none other than Trent popped into the hallway to hide from one of his friends.

We made eye contact.

I froze.

He slowly approached me, his Nerf Blaster still in hand as he walked forward. Then, I kid you not, he dramatically swung the blaster out of his hand, tossing it aside all the while maintaining eye contact with me.

I winced a little, but I could not move. He inched closer, a determination in his eye and a smirk on his face.

It was at that moment I realized. . .*I did not want to kiss Nerf Blaster guy.*

Nevertheless, he inched forward, and I stood there frozen. I *had* to try it. I had to get my first kiss out of the way. It couldn't be that bad, right?

Wrong. Bad. Very bad!

He was now standing centimeters away from me and I could smell his breath as it warmed my face, and it was not good, ladies. He had been munching on Sour Cream and Onion Ruffles all night, and I could actually still see them in his teeth.

I held back my gag reflex. *Eech!* Again, not good right before your first kiss.

He leaned forward, his arms hanging loosely in front of him like an oversized ape, his onion breath exfoliating my skin, and then he pressed his nervous, wet, Ruffle-laced lips on mine.

Apparently that was a kiss.

Please, no. Tell me that was not what kissing is like! There was no way this was what Taylor Swift had been talking about all along!

I stepped back, putting distance between us, and forced an awkward smile, my eyes scanning for an exit. To my relief, he smiled back, pausing before he turned around, grabbed the Nerf gun off the ground, and fled the scene.

That was not what I had envisioned!

The boy who just exited the hallway was *nothing* like the boy who had been texting me all along. What had happened to the boy with the smooth conversation? The effortlessly casual flirtation? The perfect word-to-emoji ratio?

The confident boy-man who had been texting me was non-existent.

Perhaps I should have spent more time with him in person.

* *

REALIZATION #38: Taking time to get to know someone IRL (in real life) can prevent some really awkward moments!

* *

ASK YOURSELF OR A FRIEND

1. Have you ever started a relationship online, through an app, or through text? How did it end?

2. Why do you think Alyssa thought Trent was so cool over text but so completely different in person?

3. What is it that people miss screen-to-screen and gain face-to-face?

4. How can you better cultivate face-to-face conversation in your current or future dating relationships?

FINAL THOUGHTS

Later that night, I received a text from Trent about how he would be dreaming of my cherry Chapstick.

I screamed in frustration and threw my phone at my bedroom wall.

I broke up with him the next week.

Poor Trent. He didn't even see it coming.

But let's face it—Text Trent was a completely different person than Trent IRL. Perhaps he had too much practice over text and not enough practice face-to-face.

CHAPTER 39

Influencer: Possibility or Fantasy?

My friend is a third-grade teacher. Every week a different one of her students gets to be the "star of the week" in her classroom. They'll show pictures, bring their favorite toys to school, and be interviewed in front of the entire class.

One of the questions she asks every kid is "What do you want to be when you grow up?"

Kids used to always answer, "A basketball player," "A fireman," "A dolphin trainer," "President of the United States". . . .

Now eight out of ten of her students say the exact same thing:

"A YouTuber!"

Eight out of ten is spot-on. Earlier in the book we shared how 86 percent of young people would like to be influencers of some sort. I realize if eight out of ten young people want to be an influencer, then there is a good chance you, as you sit here and read this, might have some aspirations to become an Insta-celeb or become a little more recognizable on YouTube. But let me ask you to step back for a minute and think about this. What if eight out of ten young people today stopped pursuing the possibilities of being a nurse, teacher, electrician, or accountant? Who is going to take their blood pressure when they go to the doctor's office? Who are all these YouTube influencers going to call when they need to install new electric outlets in their basement?

And dare I ask, how many of these influencers will actually

become successful? Eight out of ten? Five out of ten? One out of ten? Fewer?

What happens if they don't get enough followers?

How far are they willing to go to get *more* followers?

Let's look a little more closely at what influencers actually look like today and whether this desire to become a full-time influencer is a possibility or just a fantasy.

First, let me admit to you up front, I don't want to be a dream crusher. When LeBron James was ten years old and he told his friends, "I want to be in the NBA," I'm sure many of his buddies thought, *Suuuure. You just go on dreaming, Little LeBron.* But he made it happen. I think it's great to pursue your dreams with persistence and practicality (the hard work that makes it happen).

But let me also be straight with you. LeBron was one in a million. Actually, if you believe he is the "greatest of all time" (the GOAT), then he's actually more like one in 7.5 billion.

So what about influencers? Are they one in a million?

Let me focus on that word *million* for a moment, because if you are one of those eight out of ten young people who want to be an influencer for their full-time job, then let a *million* be your target, because that's literally how many followers you need. **And for those of you who have read you only need five hundred followers to get paid. . .keep reading.**

Let me break down the math. (Yes, influencers, if you want to influence, you need to do a little math. Here it is summed up in just a few paragraphs.) Here's what you need to know.

Let's say you're a gamer who wants to get money for views. On average, an established influencer who has built relationships with sponsors can receive about $3 to $5 for 1,000 YouTube views.[1] Do the math really quick. *If you get sponsored* (if is the key word here—you first have to attract a good sponsor, and those sponsorships always have strings attached about what you can say and do) and then one of your videos gets 100,000 views, you could make $500 in ad revenue *once*. If you got a million views, you could make $5,000 *once*—key word *once*, which would pay your bills for just one month at roughly the same pay your high school teacher gets (except she gets it every month).

But typically, if you aren't PewDiePie, then an average influencer will make "about 1 percent of follower counts per sponsored Instagram post, or $100 for every 10,000 followers."[2] If you have about 100,000 followers, you might start around $1,000 per sponsored post.

I know, some of you think $1,000 sounds pretty good. But remember, we're not talking about making $1,000 once or twice. We're talking about whether you can quit your job at Chipotle and do this as your full-time job. Again, do the math really quick. If you want to make as much money per year as your teacher, you'll need waaaay more than those 100,000 followers.

A good question to ask is "How many of these 'influencers' get enough posts to actually live on?" After all, some of you have read misleading articles about how even "micro-influencers" (100,000 followers or less) or "nano-influencers" (those with 500 to 5,000 followers) are making big bucks.

Big bucks is very misleading. More like *some* bucks.

Huffington Post interviewed a bunch of everyday influencers who are actually making income and asked them to break down what they really make. Most of them haven't been able to quit their day job.[3] Read that again. **Most of them haven't been able to quit their day job.**

In other words, they still work at Target, but they YouTube on the side. For the typical influencer who wasn't featured on a Kardashian show, and maybe had 15,000 to 30,000 followers, most of them made only about $3,000 to $5,000 in the entire year. Just one or two made a few thousand a month—again, what your schoolteacher makes, not what Kylie Jenner makes.

In fact, InfluencerMarketingHub interviewed a YouTuber named Dunn who started a YouTube channel with a friend and currently has over 700,000 subscribers. Dunn admitted, "Despite this success, we're just barely scraping by. . .but it's not enough to live. . . . Brands think we're too small to sponsor, but fans think we're too big for donations."[4]

InfluencerMarketingHub concluded, "Once a YouTube channel's subscriber-count reaches the millions, life becomes easier for the owners."[5]

Here are the numbers:

- *Under 100,000 followers*, maybe you make some extra income to buy that new equipment you need to film your videos.

- *Over 100,000 followers*, you have lots of sponsors and a little more money, but in most cases not enough to make a living.

- *One million followers*, you can finally quit Target and start influencing full-time.

How many people influence full-time?

Of the active 31 million YouTube channels out there with more than ten subscribers, only 16,000 of them have over a million followers.[6] That's about 1/20th of 1 percent. Instagram and other social media sites have worse odds.

Let me explain it this way: if your high school has 2,252 students, then about 1,937 of them want to be influencers, but only one will be able to make it full-time.

What's my point?

Simple: have a backup plan.

Maybe you'll be the one in 2,252 students in your school to actually get sponsored enough to be a full-time influencer. But just in case you aren't, maybe you should keep pursuing something else. If you want to be a nurse or a teacher, then keep college on your radar.

Or if you'd like to be an electrician, plumber, or X-ray technician, then you could become an intern or go to a trade school to learn those skills and be earning a solid living in just a few years.

Here's the thing: an electrician can make fun YouTube videos on the side of how to install a ceiling fan. If your videos do well enough, you can tell people to "be sure to use ACME wiring" (or whoever sponsors you) and earn a little bit of side income.

If you enjoy shooting fun videos—shoot fun videos. You never know. They might actually pay someday. Just don't quit school or close doors to other career opportunities. Always keep a backup plan in the works.

And if you're the one in 2,252 who makes a living as an influencer, I look forward to seeing your posts!

· ·

REALIZATION #39: People who want to be influencers should always keep a backup plan in the works.

· ·

ASK YOURSELF OR A FRIEND

1. Do you have a fun YouTube channel or Instagram account you enjoy? Tell me about it.

2. Would you like to be an influencer someday? If so, what would that probably look like?

3. What do you think being a successful influencer would require?

4. What is something else, besides being an influencer, that you think would be a fun career? What would this career require?

5. If 1,937 out of 2,252 young people want to be influencers, and only one is successful, how do you think this will affect the mental health of the 1,936 who don't make it?

FINAL THOUGHTS

Let's pause for a moment and consider the 1,936 people who want to be influencers but don't make it full-time.

Some of them might be content doing it as a side thing.

Some of them won't.

How do you think this will affect them?

Ask Sam Benarroch, who had about 166,000 followers on social media, but purposely took a break from it because of the anxiety he experienced when his "likes" started dropping. "Not getting the numbers that you want is so harmful. It's scary because it's this spiral of not ever feeling like you're enough, and that leaves this mental scarring. It's contributed to my mental health not being the best lately. I definitely had to get some therapy because of this."[7]

Sam is not alone.

Let's look at two noticeable side effects experts are seeing right now:

1. *Depression.* Today's young people are experiencing record levels of depression that most experts attribute to the pressurized environment social media is creating.[8] It's pretty understandable. When 86 percent of young people are desperately seeking more followers, and the overwhelming majority don't get as many as desired, their self-esteem is affected. *Why don't I have as many followers as Taylor? How come they didn't like my post?*

2. *Risky behaviors.* Since most of today's young people feel the need for more followers, they aren't using wise privacy settings and are exposing themselves to online predators.

Have you observed either of these realities with people your age?

How can you avoid these dangerous side effects?

CHAPTER 40
Reflections from a Media Minimalist

"Hi, my name is Alyssa and I am a media-aholic."

Okay, maybe I haven't exactly had to say that, but that's a little what I felt like the first month of no Instagram.

When others asked me about my Instagram or told me to look something up on social media, I had to tell them I don't have any social media anymore. And seriously, it felt a little awkward at first. People would ask me why I didn't have it anymore and I felt like I was confessing my addiction to them or something.

But then I received some reactions I didn't expect.

Kindness.

Profound interest.

Sincere questions. . .like the kind you get when someone is considering something for themselves.

Ever since I've taken the leap to quit Instagram for a year, I have had so many healthy conversations about the effects of social media. Even as we had readers screen this book, the conversations began.

"I did that too. Amazing!"

"I've been thinking of doing that. How has it been. . .really?"

My story of struggling with social media was not unique to me. And the absence of social media that started as a quiet and embarrassed confession has transformed into a proud testimony to others around me, one that many people want to hear more about.

The coolest part of it all has been the feeling that I am not alone in my decision.

I keep running into an increasing number of people around me who have made the same choice to be completely free of social media. Some of these people, I soon realized, are called "media minimalists." And yes, it kind of feels like I'm part of a hip, cutting-edge club. Not exclusive, but very trendy. And yes, people are jealous (maybe not, but just let me think so, okay?).

Here are some highlights from my new media-minimalist journey so far:

- My decision prompted several friends and family members to follow suit and delete social media from their lives. It has been so sweet to see how one decision has helped many others feel like they can let go too!

- I went driving down to lunch the other day with one of my close friends in her convertible Bug. We had our sunglasses on, the warm spring Santa Barbara wind was rushing through our hair, and we were blasting music. We laughed the entire drive, singing along to old throwback songs from our youth as we cruised along the coast. Picturesque, right? Here's the thing: Honestly, **a few months ago I would have been thinking about the perfect angle from which to capture this moment and worried about how my windblown hair looked.** But instead I enjoyed the sun and smiled at the trees that whizzed by, completely free from the pressure of sharing the moment with anyone else.

- Despite the popular belief that board games have become extinct, I've found that this belief is false! My parents taught me Euchre, a card game for four, and I have since convinced my roommates to play cards with me. We had the best night just last week, playing cards and munching on peanut butter pretzels. No screens required. One of the most fun times we've had together in a long time!

- When people tell me to look someone up, I no longer search via Instagram but via Google, and let me tell you, it is quite entertaining to see the difference between the photos brought up by Google Images and the ones on Instagram. No perfectly filtered, flawless images, but an array of candid photos, some not as glamorous as people would like to be displayed. . . . Have you ever seen Tom Cruise chilling in the pool in a fedora? Total dad vibes. Sorry, Tom, but a fedora and swim trunks? Not your best moment.

- I ran into one of our interns for our admissions office the other night, Brittney. She's the coolest girl, down-to-earth, somehow always super fashionable, and just overall chill. She had a flip phone in her hand and I gasped in exclamation, demanding she explain where she got that. She smiled big and told me she spontaneously decided to switch out her smartphone for it last weekend. Turns out she was just done with all the pressures of social media. She shared her story, I shared mine, and now we're gonna grab lunch together. Total bonding moment. I love finding others in my unspoken minimalist club!

The last few months have been so great for me; I've never felt freer. But I want to emphasize that I'm not harping on having a phone—I still have one and enjoy using it! Phones are simply tools. We're the ones who decide how to use them, whether for our harm or for our good. May we continually strive to do the latter!

REALIZATION #40: Life as a media minimalist is surprisingly freeing.

ASK YOURSELF OR A FRIEND

1. Have you encountered others who have taken a break from media? What do you think of them?

2. List all the negatives you can think of when *not* having social media—for example, what will you miss out on?

3. Would it really be so bad to have to deal with these negatives?

4. Why do you think Alyssa expressed herself as feeling "free"?

5. What is one way you can change your consumption of social media to make you feel freer from it?

FINAL THOUGHTS

It has been just five months, almost halfway through my social media fast, and time has flown by. I'm honestly shocked to think it has already been so long, because social media has barely been on my mind. But that is the greatest realization—the most freeing aspect of this break I'm taking!

Minimalism isn't just for the hipsters after all!

Alyssa and Jonathan Write...
Looking Back

As we wrap up our thoughts and look back at all of these realizations, we decided to show you the raw dialogue the two of us had after writing *The Teen's Guide to Face-to-Face Connections in a Screen-to-Screen World.*

Jonathan: I can honestly say that this has been one of the most rewarding experiences writing a book I've ever had.

Alyssa: And you've written *a lot* of books.

Jonathan: Yeah, but never with my Ditta!

Alyssa: (*Blushing noticeably*) Dad. You can't call me that anymore—I'm twenty-four years old!!

Jonathan: It's your nickname! It was meant as a term of endearment. That's a good thing, Lyssy.

Alyssa: Okay, okay, thanks. But still... (*Still blushing*)

Jonathan: Ha-ha. But honestly, this was such a fun book to write. First, because it was fun collaborating with you, and second, because I felt like the subject was something so real and relevant to our everyday experiences. I mean, we both have multiple screens, we use them to connect with family and friends, and we also enjoy the entertainment those screens provide. But at the same time, we've seen these screens distract us from what's important. So in essence, this book has been a collection of confessions and discoveries (dare I say "realizations") that have impacted us greatly, and we simply hope other people can learn from our discoveries. . .*and mistakes.*

Alyssa: I totally agree. I honestly feel like writing this book has helped me improve my screen usage so much more! And it has also sparked conversations with others in my life who have observed their own screen usage. It has been so meaningful to be able to reflect together with them. I don't think I have ever been so aware of how screens have affected me until I reflected back on the input of screens throughout the last ten to fifteen years of my life. . .man, I'm getting old.

Jonathan: Ha! Well, let's just say you're getting wise. And sincerely, you did an amazing job speaking honestly throughout these pages, even sharing a few moments from your past that were probably pretty hard to reveal. Everyone who screened this book (over one hundred people) was so moved and encouraged, not only by your authenticity, but by your insight and real-world application.

Alyssa: Well, thank you, truly. It means so much to hear you and others respond to my story so positively. It wasn't easy to share at first, but I'm glad I did. It was actually really cathartic!

Jonathan: That's a pretty big word.

Alyssa: Ha, true. But I looked it up and it really exemplifies what I want to communicate. Writing this book was therapeutic. Cleansing. Actually liberating. It helped me process my emotions and think about my relationships.

Jonathan: I'm really glad to hear that.

Alyssa: But I have to say, I don't know how you write so much, Mr. 27 Books, or however many you're up to now. By the end of this book I'm cleaned out of any stories I could possibly share. Ha-ha.

Jonathan: You'd be surprised how many more you have. They happen every day. And on behalf of all your readers, who are now "Alyssa McKee" fans, I hope to see you write more.

I Wish I Knew: Confessions of Alyssa
1. Jonathan McKee, "The Newest on Teens, Social Media and Technology," The Source for Parents, July 24, 2018, https://jonathanmckeewrites.com/archive/2018/07/24/the-newest-on-teens-social-media-technology.
2. "Social Media, Social Life: Teens Reveal Their Experiences," Common Sense Media, September 10, 2018, https://www.commonsensemedia.org/social-media-social-life-infographic.
3. Jonathan McKee, "But Mom, I Really Need My Phone in My Bedroom," The Source for Parents, June 19, 2019, https://thesource4parents.com/parenting-help/but-mom-i-really-need-my-phone-in-my-bedroom.
4. McKee, "But Mom."
5. McKee, "But Mom."
6. Christine Erickson, "A Brief History of Text Messaging," Mashable, September 21, 2012, https://mashable.com/2012/09/21/text-messaging-history.
7. Steve Jobs, "iPhone Keynote 2007," European Rhetoric, http://www.european-rhetoric.com/analyses/ikeynote-analysis-iphone/transcript-2007.
8. "Mobile Fact Sheet," Pew Research Center, June 12, 2019, https://www.pewresearch.org/internet/fact-sheet/mobile.
9. "The History of Instagram," Instazood, May 17, 2020, https://instazood.com/blog/the-history-of-instagram.

Chapter 1: Senior Cut Day
1. Trevor Haynes, "Dopamine, Smartphones and You: A Battle for Your Time," Harvard University Science in the News blog, May 1, 2018, http://sitn.hms.harvard.edu/flash/2018/dopamine-smartphones-battle-time.
2. David R. Smith, "Exactly How Many Hours Are Teens on Their Screens?" The Source for Parents, November 10, 2019, https://thesource4parents.com/youth-culture-window/exactly-how-many-hours-are-teens-on-their-screens.
3. Tom Butts, "Nielsen: U.S. Adults Spend Majority of Waking Hours Interacting with Media," TV Technology, July 1, 2019, https://www.tvtechnology.com/news/nielsen-u-s-adults-spend-majority-of-waking-hours-interacting-with-media.

Chapter 2: Connected Disconnect
1. Jean M. Twenge, "Have Smartphones Destroyed a Generation?" The Atlantic, September 2017, https://www.theatlantic.com/magazine/archive/2017/09/has-the-smartphone-destroyed-a-generation/534198.
2. David R. Smith, "Exactly How Many Hours Are Teens on Their Screens?" The Source for Parents, November 10, 2019, https://thesource4parents.com/youth-culture-window/exactly-how-many-hours-are-teens-on-their-screens.
3. Twenge, "Have Smartphones Destroyed a Generation?"

Chapter 3: Less Is More
1. Jingjing Jiang, "How Teens and Parents Navigate Screen Time and Device Distractions," Pew Research Center, August 22, 2018, https://www.pewresearch.org/internet/2018/08/22/how-teens-and-parents-navigate-screen-time-and-device-distractions.
2. Jiang, "How Teens and Parents Navigate Screen Time."
3. "Teen Smartphone Addiction National Survey 2018," Screen Education, 2018, https://www.screeneducation.org/uploads/1/1/6/6/116602217/teen_smartphone_addiction_national_survey_2018_report_6.21.18_upload_version_1.2.pdf.

Chapter 5: In 30 to 60 Days
1. "Empathy: College Students Don't Have as Much as They Used To," University of Michigan News, May 27, 2010, https://news.umich.edu/empathy-college-students-don-t-have-as-much-as-they-used-to.

Chapter 9: The Chainsaw
1. Katie Golem, "How Your Smartphone Might Sabotage Your Relationship," Gottman Institute, January 8, 2018, https://www.gottman.com/blog/smartphone-might-sabotage-relationship.
2. "Baylor Study: Cellphones Can Damage Romantic Relationships, Lead to Depression," Baylor University, September 29, 2015, https://www.baylor.edu/mediacommunications/news.php?action=story&story=161554.
3. Kelly Wynne, "Social Media Is at the Center of Most Divorces, Divorce Attorney Says in New Book," *Newsweek*, December 9, 2018, https://www.newsweek.com/social-media-center-most-divorces-divorce-attorney-says-new-book-1251208.

Chapter 11: You're Fired
1. Jon Ronson, "How One Stupid Tweet Blew Up Justine Sacco's Life," *New York Times Magazine*, February 12, 2015, https://www.nytimes.com/2015/02/15/magazine/how-one-stupid-tweet-ruined-justine-saccos-life.html.
2. Samantha Schmidt, "Harvard Withdraws 10 Acceptances for 'Offensive' Memes in Private Group Chat," *Philadelphia Inquirer*, June 5, 2017, https://www.inquirer.com/philly/education/Harvard-withdraws-10-acceptances-for-offensive-memes-in-private-group-chat.html.

Chapter 13: Power Outage
1. Screen Education, "Gen-Z Relieved to Escape Their Smartphones for Several Weeks, Study Suggests," PR Newswire, March 19, 2018, https://www.prnewswire.com/news-releases/gen-z-relieved-to-escape-their-smartphones-for-several-weeks-study-suggests-300615600.html.
2. Screen Education, "Gen-Z Relieved."
3. Screen Education, "Gen-Z Relieved."

Chapter 14: Talk to Me
1. "Porn in the Digital Age: New Research Reveals 10 Trends," Barna, April 6, 2016, http://barna.org/research/porn-in-the-digital-age-new-research-reveals-10-trends.

Chapter 15: Talk, Text, FaceTime, Call
1. Lauren E. Sherman, Minas Michikyan, and Patricia M. Greenfield, "The Effects of Text, Audio, Video, and In-Person Communication on Bonding between Friends," *Cyberpsychology: Journal of Psychosocial on Cyberspace* 7, no. 2 (2013), https://cyberpsychology.eu/article/view/4285/3330.

Chapter 16: I Wish My Family Did That
1. Alexis C. Madrigal, "When Did TV Watching Peak?" *The Atlantic*, May 30, 2018, https://www.theatlantic.com/technology/archive/2018/05/when-did-tv-watching-peak/561464/.
2. "The Benefits of the Family Table," American College of Pediatricians, May

2014, https://www.acpeds.org/the-college-speaks/position-statements/parenting-issues/the-benefits-of-the-family-table.

Chapter 19: Fire
1. Tony Bizjak, Sophia Bollag, and Ryan Sabalow, "PG&E Caused Camp Fire That Destroyed Paradise and Killed 85, Cal Fire Says," *Sacramento Bee*, May 15, 2019, https://www.sacbee.com/news/local/article230445554.

Chapter 21: Ed Sheeran
1. McKenna Aiello, "Ed Sheeran Reflects on Going Two Years without a Cell Phone and His Famous Digital Detox," E! News, December 13, 2017, https://www.eonline.com/news/899954/ed-sheeran-reflects-on-going-two-years-without-a-cell-phone-and-his-famous-digital-detox.
2. Aiello, "Ed Sheeran."

Chapter 23: DM Me
1. Sarah Min, "86% of Young Americans Want to Become a Social Media Influencer," CBS News, November 8, 2019, https://www.cbsnews.com/news/social-media-influencers-86-of-young-americans-want-to-become-one.
2. "How Much Gen Z Cares about Online Celebrities, in 5 Stats," YPulse, September 24, 2019, https://www.ypulse.com/article/2019/09/24/how-much-gen-z-cares-about-online-celebrities-in-5-stats.

Chapter 25: A Minute
1. Minyvonne Burke, "Hailey Bieber Says Social Media Is 'Breeding Ground for Cruelty,'" NBC News, January 4, 2020, https://www.nbcnews.com/pop-culture/pop-culture-news/hailey-baldwin-says-social-media-breeding-ground-cruelty-n1110466.
2. Mary Meisenzahl, "Lizzo Is Quitting Twitter Because It Has 'Too Many Trolls,'" Business Insider, January 6, 2020, https://www.businessinsider.com/lizzo-quits-twitter-because-it-has-too-many-trolls-2020-1.
3. Olivia Singh, "Pete Davidson Deleted All His Instagram Posts after Clashing with Fiancée Ariana Grande's Fans," Insider, July 23, 2018, https://www.insider.com/pete-davidson-deletes-instagram-photos-videos-clashing-with-ariana-grande-fans-2018-7.
4. Margy Rochlin, "Selena Gomez (and Others) on Adapting '13 Reasons Why' for Netflix," *New York Times*, https://www.nytimes.com/2017/03/22/arts/television/selena-gomez-thirteen-reasons-why-netflix.html.
5. Talia Lakritz, "Meghan Markle Just Pulled the Ultimate Royal Move and Deleted All Her Social Media Accounts," Insider, January 9, 2018, https://www.insider.com/meghan-markle-deletes-facebook-twitter-instagram-2018-1.
6. Josh Constine, "Instagram to Test Hiding Like Counts in US, Which Could Hurt Influencers," TechCrunch, November 8, 2019, https://techcrunch.com/2019/11/08/instagram-hide-likes-us/.
7. Blake Bakkila, "She's Back! Kendall Jenner Returns to Instagram One Week after Deleting Account," *People*, November 20, 2016, https://people.com/celebrity/kendall-jenner-returns-instagram.

Chapter 27: Shaq and Kobe
1. Ron Dicker, "Shaquille O'Neal and Kobe Bryant Exchange Disses Like Old

Times," *HuffPost*, https://www.huffpost.com/entry/shaquille-oneal-kobe-bry-ant-feud_n_5d67b731e4b01fcc690fd106?guccounter=1.

2. Carly Ledbetter, "Shaquille O'Neal Is Making a Major Life Change after Kobe Bryant's Death," *HuffPost*, January 28, 2020, https://www.huffpost.com/entry/shaquille-oneal-kobe-bryant-life-change_n_5e30434fc5b6d34ea10561c5.

3. Althea Legaspi, "Shaquille O'Neal on Kobe Bryant's Death: 'I Haven't Felt a Pain That Sharp in a While,' " *Rolling Stone*, January 29, 2020, https://www.rollingstone.com/culture/culture-news/shaquille-oneal-kobe-bryant-death-944756.

4. Sam Quinn, "Shaquille O'Neal Opens Up about Kobe Bryant's Death, Rela-tionship: 'I Wish That I Could Say Something to Him,' " CBS Sports, January 29, 2020, https://www.cbssports.com/nba/news/shaquille-oneal-opens-up-about-kobe-bryants-death-relationship-i-wish-that-i-could-say-something-to-him.

Chapter 29: From Opposite Sides of the Planet

1. https://www.commonsensemedia.org/sites/default/files/uploads/pdfs/2020_surveymonkey-key-findings-toplines-teens-and-coronavirus.pdf

Chapter 32: Attack of the Killer Squirrels

1. Alina Bradford, "Squirrels: Diet, Habits and Other Facts," Live Science, June 27, 2014, https://www.livescience.com/28182-squirrels.html.

Chapter 33: Zzzzzzzz

1. Heather Monroe, "The Importance of Sleep for Teen Mental Health," *U.S. News & World Report*, July 2, 2018, https://health.usnews.com/health-care/for-better/articles/2018-07-02/the-importance-of-sleep-for-teen-mental-health.

2. Judith Owens, "Insufficient Sleep in Adolescents and Young Adults: An Update on Causes and Consequences," *Pediatrics* 134, no. 3 (September 2014), https://pediatrics.aappublications.org/content/134/3/e921.

3. Amy Green, "Should Bedrooms Be No-Phone Zones for Teens?" Psychology Today, February 17, 2017, https://www.psychologytoday.com/us/blog/psy-curious/201702/should-bedrooms-be-no-phone-zones-teens.

4. Jonathan McKee, "But Mom, I Really Need My Phone in My Bedroom," The Source for Parents, June 19, 2019, https://thesource4parents.com/parenting-help/but-mom-i-really-need-my-phone-in-my-bedroom.

5. Jean Twenge, "Analysis: Teens Are Sleeping Less. Why? Smartphones," PBS, October 19, 2017, https://www.pbs.org/newshour/science/analysis-teens-are-sleeping-less-why-smartphones.

6. American Academy of Pediatrics, "Sexuality, Contraception, and the Media," *Pediatrics* 126, no. 3 (September 2010), https://pediatrics.aappublications.org/content/126/3/576.full.

7. American Academy of Pediatrics, "Media Use in School-Age Children and Adolescents," *Pediatrics* 138, no. 5 (November 2016), https://pediatrics.aappublications.org/content/138/5/e20162592.

8. National Sleep Foundation, "Teens and Sleep," SleepFoundation.org, https://www.sleepfoundation.org/articles/teens-and-sleep.

9. "The Impact of Sleep on Teen Mental Health," Georgetown Behavioral Health Institute, December 1, 2017, https://www.georgetownbehavioral.com/node/1767.

10. Monroe, "Importance of Sleep for Teen Mental Health."

11. Quoted in Niraj Chokshi, "Your Kids Think You're Addicted to Your Phone," *New York Times*, May 29, 2019, https://www.nytimes.com/2019/05/29/technology/cell-phone-usage.html.

Chapter 35: Five Songs That Make You Think
1. Victoria Rideout and Michael B. Robb, *The Common Sense Census: Media Use by Tweens and Teens, 2019* (San Francisco: Common Sense Media, 2019), https://www.commonsensemedia.org/sites/default/files/uploads/research/2019-census-8-to-18-key-findings-updated.pdf.

Chapter 39: Influencer: Possibility or Fantasy?
1. Influencer Marketing, "How Much Do YouTubers Make? A YouTuber's Pocket Guide," Influencer MarketingHub, April 28, 2020, https://influencermarketinghub.com/how-much-do-youtubers-make.
2. Cara Kelly, "Fyre Festival to Fashion Week, How Do Instagram Influencers Make So Much Money?" *USA Today*, February 12, 2019, https://www.usatoday.com/story/news/investigations/2019/02/12/instagram-youtube-influencer-rates-fyre-festival-fashion-week-money-rich-branding-ads-girls/2787560002.
3. Joline Buscemi, "Here's How Much Money These 7 Influencers Actually Make, and How," *HuffPost*, December 18, 2019, https://www.huffpost.com/entry/how-much-influencers-make_l_5dee68a6e4b05d1e8a556bbc.
4. Quoted in Influencer Marketing, "How Much Do YouTubers Make?"
5. Influencer Marketing, "How Much Do YouTubers Make?"
6. Matthias Funk, "How Many YouTube Channels Are There?" January 31, 2020, https://www.tubics.com/blog/number-of-youtube-channels/.
7. Rebecca Jennings, "Tikked Off: What Happens When TikTok Fame Fades," Vox, February 27, 2020, https://www.vox.com/the-goods/2020/2/27/21153364/tiktok-famous-backlash.
8. Jonathan McKee, "Building the Self-Esteem of Generation-Screen," The Source for Parents, July 24, 2019, https://thesource4parents.com/parenting-help/building-the-self-esteem-of-generation-screen.

INTERESTING FACTS SOURCES
* https://www.thefire.org/catching-up-with-coddling-part-two-trigger-warnings-screen-time-v-social-media-covid-19-and-the-continuing-decline-of-gen-zs-mental-health/
*Quoted in Zak Cheney-Rice, "One of the First Viral Facebook Videos Turns 10 Years Old," Mic, February 12, 2014, https://www.mic.com/articles/82055/one-of-the-first-viral-facebook-videos-turns-10-years-old.
*Victoria Rideout and Michael B. Robb, The Common Sense Census: Media Use by Tweens and Teens, 2019 (San Francisco: Common Sense Media, 2019), https://www.commonsensemedia.org/sites/default/files/uploads/research/2019-census-8-to-18-key-findings-updated.pdf.
*Unemployment Rates and Earnings by Educational Attainment," U.S. Bureau of Labor Statistics, September 4, 2019, https://www.bls.gov/emp/chart-unemployment-earnings-education.htm